Henry Reed Stiles

Letters From the Prisons and Prison-Ships of the Revolution

With Notes

Henry Reed Stiles

Letters From the Prisons and Prison-Ships of the Revolution
With Notes

ISBN/EAN: 9783744754699

Printed in Europe, USA, Canada, Australia, Japan

Cover: Foto ©Suzi / pixelio.de

More available books at **www.hansebooks.com**

LETTERS

FROM THE

PRISONS AND PRISON-SHIPS

OF THE

REVOLUTION.

WITH NOTES

BY HENRY R. STILES, M. D.

NEW YORK:

PRIVATELY PRINTED.

1865.

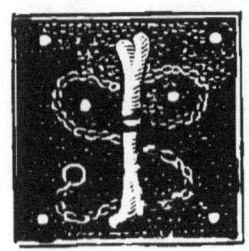ONATHAN GILLET, the writer of the following letter, was born in Weſt Hartford,[1] Conn., February 4, 1738, and was by occupation a farmer. He early enliſted in the Revolutionary army, where he held a rank, although of what grade, is not now known.[2] He was with his regiment on Long Iſland, at the time of the Battle of Long Iſland, Auguſt 27th, 1776, and at the retreat of the American army, after that defeat, was one of a ſquad of eight men, who, in conſequence of a ſcarcity of boats, were captured by the enemy before they could embark.[3] He

was firft confined in the prifon-fhip, but through the influence of JOHN ARCHER,[*] a Mafonic brother, was releafed from there, and obtained the liberty of the city on parole. For two years he remained a prifoner in New York, and finally, in 1780, when his health became fo broken down as to preclude the poffibility of his long furviving, he was permitted to return to his friends and home at Weft Hartford, where he died, within a few weeks, manifefting (as it is faid) every fymptom of having been poifoned, as well as ftarved.

During his laft ficknefs he faid to his fon, Jonathan, Jr., who was watching by his bedfide, " The war may continue many years, and fhould you enlift, or be called into the United States fervice, you may be taken prifoner and carried to New York. If fo, I would have you inquire for Mr. JOHN ARCHER, a man with whom I boarded after I came from the prifon-fhip, and he will affift you." Singular as it may appear, all thefe incidents, as fuggefted by the dying man, did actually occur. The fon, after his father's death, enlifted in the fervice, was taken prifoner at Horfe Neck,[5] by Col. Delancey's[6] Light Horfe, and Robertfon's Corps of Light Infantry—was taken to New York, and imprifoned, as his father had been before him, in the Old Sugar Houfe.[7]

Bethinking himfelf, in his trouble, of his father's dying inftructions, he took means to notify Mr. Archer of his whereabouts, and who he was. Mr. A. came to the windows of the prifon, and inquired for him, and frequently furnifhed him fuch things as he required during his imprifonment. His account of the fufferings of thofe confined in this prifon, as he was accuftomed to relate them to his friends, in after-

life, was full of horror and intereſt. Mice, in-
ſeĉts, and anything that was an apology for food
was ſpcedily devoured to keep them for a time
from the horrors of ſtarvation. Mr. Gillet
mentioned among other things, that the dry
parings of a turnip, which he accidently found,
in one of his paroxyſms of hunger, was the
ſweeteſt morſel that he ever ate in his life. A
few years beforc his death, (which occurred at
Canaan, Conn.) Mr. JONATHAN GILLET, Jr.,
received a cane made from the timbers of the
Old Sugar Houſe—being at that time one of the
four oldeſt ſurvivors of the priſoners who have
been confincd in that den of horrors.[3]

My Friends,

No doubt my misfortunes have reached your
ears. Sad as it is, it is true as fad. I was made
prifoner the 27 day of Auguft paft by a people
called hefhens[9] and by a party called Yagers,[10]
the moft Inhuman of all mortals I cant give
Room to picture them here; but thus much I at
firft Refolved not to be taken but by the Imper-
tunity of the Seven taken with me[11] and being
forounded on all fides by numbers I unhappily
furenderd; would to God I never had—then I
fhould never (have) known there unmercifull cruelties; they firft difarmed me then plundred me
of all I had, watch Buckles money and fum
Clothing[12] after which they abufed me by brufing
my flefh with the buts of their (guns. They
knocked me down;) I got up and they (kept
on) beating me almoft all the way to there
(camp) where I go fhot of them—the next

thing was I was allmoſt ſtarved to death by
them. I was keept here 8 days (then) ſent on
board a ſhip, where I continued 39 days and
by much worſe than when on ſhore after I
was ſet on   at New Yorke confined
a ſtrong guard till the (20th) day of November
after which I have had my liberty to walk part
over the City between ſun and ſun, notwithſtand-
ing there generous allowance of proviſion I muſt
inevitably have periſhed with hunger had not
ſum friends in this (city) Relieved my extreme
neceſſity but I cant expect they can always do it—
what I ſhall do next I know not being naked for
cloths and void of money and winter preſent,
and proviſions very ſkerce freſh meat one ſhilling
per pound Butter three ſhillings pr pound
Cheeſe two ſhillings Turnips and potatoes at a
ſhilling half-peck milk fifteen Coppers a quart—
bread equally as dear; & the General ſays he

cant find us fuel thro' the winter tho at prefent
we Recieve fum cole.

I was after put on board fiezed violantly with
the difentarry[13]—it followed me hard upwards of
fix weeks—after that a flow fever, but now I
am vaftly better—I pray thefe lines might find
you and your children in health and fhould be
glad to here from you if pofably—My finfeare
love to you and my children—may God keep
and preferve you at all times from fin & ficknefs
and death—May he feed and cloth you but above
all prepare you all to appeare before his righteous (bar, that you might each of you) Render your accounts with Joy: my being ab-
fent from you I hope dont hinder your being
mindful of your fouls welfare; nor my fuffering
take your thoughts from your duty to God;
never murmur nor Repine at the hand of providence what God doth—Remember it is Right—

teach your Children the paths of Virtue, and to walk therein ; may they Remember there Creator in the days of there youth, and live to do much good in there day and generation—may you have the prefence of God with you to enable and affift you in this important worke—I leve you all, if alive, in the hands of a merciful God who will have mercy on all that feek him, and may you be of that happy number whofe God is the Lord, and when you quit this mortal fhore may you Reach a far better, where Sorrow and Vexatious troubles never come.

After giving you a fmall fketch of myfelf and troubles I will Endeavor to faintly lead you into the poor cituation the foldiers are in efpechally thofe taken at long Ifland where I was ; in fact there cafes are deplorable and they are Real objects of pitty—they are ftill confined and in houfes where there is no fire—poor mortals, with little or no cloths, perifhing with hunger, offering 8 dollars in paper for one in filver to Relieve their diftrefling hunger: oca-fioned for want of food there natures are brook and gone, fome almoft loofe their voices and fome there hearing—they are crouded into churches and there guarded night and day. I cant paint the horable appearance they make—it is fhock-ing to human nature to behold them. Could I draw the curtain from before you; there expofe to your view a lean Jaw^d. mortal   hunger laid his fkinney hand and whet to keeneft Edge his ftomach cravings, forounded with tattred gar-ments, Rotten Raggs clofe befet with unwel-comed vermin. Could I do this, I fay—pof- , fable I might in fome (fmall) manner fix your Idea with what appearance fum hundreds of thefe poor creatures make in houfes where once people attempted to Implore God's Blefsings &c.[14] but I muft fay no more of there calami-

ties. God be merciful to them—I cant afford them no Relief—If I had money I foon would do it, but I have none for myfelf—I wrote
to you by Major Wells to try and fee if fome one would help me to hard money under my prefent neceffity I (could) write no more if I had the General would not allow it to go out & if ever you write to me I would have you write very fhort or elfe I fhall never fee it &c. I have going on due to me of wages fix months when Completed will be upwards of a Hundred dollars which I am fuffering for a part now, and if any one will help me to fum money now, I in this Impower you to Give them an Order on Capt" Hubbard who hath fum of my money now in his hands which order may fecure them— it was when in the caufe of my country I per- took of this misfortune, and will none ftep forth to help make my life fome fmall matter com- fortable while I Live. I have little or no expecta-

tion of being Releafed from this my Prefent
Confinement during the conteft, at leaft not
under a year from this but fhould I be fo happy
as to meet with a quick Releafe I foon would
attack my old friends the hefhens and try hard
to be Revenged on them for my two Eyes and
Give them full proof I never would be Taken
again for I never fhall forget the Roberys, blows
and Infults I met with as well as hunger, Since
they are Imprinted in fo Legable carraters on
my memory during my Reafon—what they
Robed me of that day would with a moderate
computation amounted to the value of feventy
two dollars at leaft and how much fince I cant
tell.

Turn on another fide and Read on if you can
the Rege' * * * I will give you as near an
exact account how many prifoners the enemy
have taken as I can—They took on Long Ifland
of Huntington Regiment 64, and of officers

40; [15] of other regiments about 60; they took on Montozin Island [16] 14; they took on Stratton Island [17] 7 men; they took at Fort Washington [18] 2200 officers and men. They took on the Jersey side about 28 officers and men belonging to the army. So in all it amounted to 3135 officers and men, and how many killed I dont know, Many died of there wounds; and as before mentioned we have lost of those that went out with me, of sickness occasioned by hunger 8, and more lie at the point of death. We lost two sergeants, and how many since (we) land (ed) cant Rightly say but I believe at least one third part but notwithstanding this we are not discouraged yet &c. Roger Filer hath lost one of his legs and part of a Thigh it was his left. John Moody died here a prisoner.

So Now to conclude my little Ragged History will be in a few words, I as you know ever

did Imprefs on your mind to look to God for
fo ftill I continue to do the fame—think lefs of
me but more of your Creator—Remember (you
are born to die, and you could not but expect to
meet) with troubles.   Ware it Gods will I fhould
be glad to fee you and the children before I am
called to Depart this life, but if I dont I fhant
allow myfelf to be uneafy, for a complaining
uneafy temper of foul carries punifhment along
with it.   So I exort you to fhun that folly.

So in this I wifh you well and bid you fare-
well, and fubfcribe myfelf your neareft friend
and well wifher for Ever.

JOHN^ GILLET.

Tell Co. not to forget   my fincere Love to you
her dad for he hant   and the children.[19]
forget her.

N. B. My deuty to father & mother my Love
to Brothers & Sifters neighbours and friends

Eſpeſhally B. Colton Eſqʳ. Mr. Collens, Mr.
Croſby &c.

New York December 2ⁿᵈ 1776.

To

ELIZᴬ GILLET

at Weſt Hartford."

(*Endorſed*)

" To

Mrs. ELIZABETH GILLET,

at Weſt Hartford."

(Postmark on the above letter.)

Apt. STEPHEN BUCK-
LAND, the writer of the fol-
lowing letters, was of Eaſt
Hartford,[20] Conn., and commanded a privateer. He was,
however, taken a priſoner, and, with his officers
and crew, confined in the "Old Jerſey"[21] from
which theſe letters were written.

To Mrs. Mary Buckland.

PRISON-SHIP OF NEW YORK,
April 22d, 1782.

My Dear:

Before this comes to hand you will doubtleſs
hear of our misfortune. I have nothing to write,

but that we are all well, except fome have got the fmall-pox. Poor Michael was drowned by the overfetting of the boat, and feveral others in great danger.

I hope it won't be long before will get home by fome means or other. Give yourfelf no uneafinefs about me, I live very well, and

Remain your ever affectionate

STEPHEN BUCKLAND.

Mrs. Buckland.

TO AARON OLMSTED, CAPT. GIDEON OLMSTED, and ABRAHAM MILLER.

On board the PRISON-SHIP, NEW YORK,
April 9th, 1782.

SIRS:

Before this comes to hand you will doubtlefs hear of our fate. We were taken the 2d inft., by the Brig *Perfeverance,*[22] Rofs, Commander. Ezekiel Olmfted is flightly wounded, but will be

well in a few days. All the reft are well. Poor
Michael was drowned by the over-fetting of the
boat, and feveral others narrowly efcaped. Our
fituation you can guefs. If you can do anything
for us, fhould be glad. If you get any perfon to
exchange for any of us, you muft get him or
them paroled, and fend them in on condition
that they get the perfons exchanged that you fend
them for, or to return; for you fend ever fo
many in a flag, they will not be exchanged for
us. Remember me to my family and friends.

I remain, Sirs, yours,

STEPHEN BUCKLAND.

Mr. Aaron Olmfted, ⎫
Capt. Gideon Olmfted, ⎬   .
Mr. Abraham Miller. ⎭

P. S. April 22d, Efq. Legerd was on board
yefterday, and informs us that there will be no
exchange for privateerfmen, that he had got

3

liberty to take twenty prifoners only, that were taken in merchantmen. Our fituation is truly diftreffing, efpecially our people, for they were ftripped of everything, even to the buckles out of their fhoes, and buttons out of their fhirts, hats, coats and jackets. Many of them have got the fmall-pox, and muft all have it that han't had it, and have not a farthing of money. You would do well to inform their friends that if they are inclined to fend them any relief they may if an opportunity prefents. There is on board this fhip about feven hundred prifoners, and increafing almoft every day. You can eafily guefs what a life we muft live, and hot weather coming on. At prefent we are as well as can be expected. What provifion we get is very good. It is an excellent place to prepare a man for inoculation. Lieut. Warner ftayed in the brig that took us and had the promife of being fet afhore. I hope he has got home before this.

If you can think of any way by which you can get us out, fhould be very glad. For my part, I cant think of any at prefent, but to make the beft of a bad bargain.

STEPHEN BUCKLAND.

Mr. Aaron Olmfted, one of the parties thus addreffed, was a brother-in-law of Capt. Buckland, and a brother of the Ezekiel Olmfted, mentioned in the letter, as "flightly wounded," &c. As foon as poffible he vifited the *Jerfey* Prifonfhip, under a flag, to afcertain what could be done to relieve or to mitigate the fufferings of his relatives. But he found that Death had anticipated his errand of mercy. Capt. Buckland had died on the 7th of May, being in the 36th year of his age, and his brother Ezekiel had died about the fame time, aged 26 years. The latter, in the laft hours of his life, fent his gold fleeve buttons to the lady to whom he was betrothed. Mr. Olmſted, had the pleaſure of relieving Captains White and Flagg of Eaſt Hartford, and of returning them to their homes and families.

EVI HANFORD, the fon of
Levi Hanford, was born at
Norwalk, Conn.,[23] on the 19th
of February, 1759, enlifted in
the militia in 1775, and in 1776
was in the fervice at New York. In March,
1777, being then a member of a company commanded by Capt. Seth Seymour,[24] he was, with
twelve others,[25] under Lt. J. B. Eels, captured
by the Britifh, at a place called the "Old Well,"
in South Norwalk. On removal to New York,
he was confined fucceffively in the Quaker Meeting Houfe and other Hofpitals,[26] and afterwards
upon the prifon-fhip "Good Intent."[27] He
was releafed from captivity on the 8th of May,
1778, and of his fubfequent life the reader may

learn from the interefting Narrative of his Life
and Adventures, published by CHAS. I. BUSH-
NELL, Esq., in 1863.   Mr. Hanford fubfequently
married Mary, the daughter of Gen. John Mead,
of Horfeneck, Conn., and died October 19th,
1854, being at the time one of the four oldeft
furvivors of the Prifons and Prifon-fhips of the
Revolution.

The following letter, written by him to his
father, while a prifoner at the Old Sugar Houfe,
in Liberty ftreet, has been furnifhed to us by
the courtefy of Mr. Bufhnell, and is a literal
copy of the original.   In confequence of his
weak and debilitated condition, having juft re-
covered from ficknefs, he was obliged to get a
friend to commence the letter for him—but it
was afterwards completed by his own hand.   The
line between the two portions of the letter—and
reproduced from the original—fhow the portions
which each wrote.

" New York June 7ᵗʰ 1777.

" Loving Father.

I take the opportunity to let you know that I am alive and in reasonable health, since I had the small-pox—thanks be to the Lord for it, and hoping these lines will find you well, and all the family—my kindest love to you and my Brothers and sisters and to my friends and neighbors all, and no more at present—But I remain Your loving son   Levi Hanford, till death—

———   — .. —

I received the things You sent to me.

We have sent a petition to our Governor,[28] and wish you would go and see if you cant get us exchanged—if you please—Matthias Comstock is dead — Samuel Husted, Ebenezer Hoyt[29] Jonathan Kellog has gone to the hospital to be enoculated to day—they want money very much

—I have been fick but hope I am better—there is a doctor here that has helpt me, which coft me fomething—I would not go to the Hofpital, for all manner of difeafes prevail there. I would that You would fend me fome money when You can. I fhall want very much—Danbury Prifoners are going home—they petitioned to our government and they have got out, and we have done the fame, and do, if you can poffibly help us, do you fend to the Governor and try to help us. I dont expect to fee home foon—Be fure to fend to us—Should be glad to hear from You. Remember my kind love to all my friends—I am Your Obedient fon

LEVI HANFORD.

I received from Colonel Hart[30] £4—4—6."

 HE following *Lines* were lately *written* by a *Prisoner* in the *Provost* at *Newport*. Please to publish them, if you think them worthy of a place in your Gazette.

J. H.

" Within these Walls fair freedom's sons immur'd,
Have Want, Distress and Insult, long endur'd,
Yet undismay'd, determin'd to the end,
Their bleeding country's Honor to defend ;
They curse the Tyrant, and deride his Pow'r,
Who meant their Land by Locusts to devour,
Piniard their Rights, and riot as their spoil,
Degrade their Senators, their Wives defile,

4

Shake down the Bulwark of their *honeſt Fame*,
And divide the Eſſence of their very Name;
Laugh at the Idiot's threat, tho' ermin'd o'er,
To dye their happy Fields with crimſon Gore
Conſume their Dwellings, cruſh their floating Trade,
Entomb their Liberties and damn their Shade,
America reſolved to be free,
Spurns at the Wretch and kens his Deſtiny."

New Hampſhire Gazette, Tues., Jan. 19, 1779.

———

Salem, Auguſt 14.

Meſſrs. Printers,

By publiſhing the following extract from a letter, written by a captain of an American privateer, while on board a priſon ſhip in New York you will oblige many of your readers and particularly your humble ſervant,

G. M.

" This may ferve to inform you that I was taken thirty five hours out of Cafco Bay, and brought to New York, where I can neither find friends nor money. It is very fickly here—one third of my crew is fick, and all the reft are likely to be fo. There is not more than one in five that recovers. I fee my brave companions dying daily like rotten fheep, only for want of a little attention in our people in taking care of, and fending the prifoners they take from time to time, in order to be exchanged, without fome mode of relief, many a brave man is loft to his family, friends and country.

There is now 200 out of 6, fuffering the pains of this ficknefs, and its daily increafing. I would requeft you to acquaint my friends to forward an exchange with all difpatch poffible.

All the New London men are exchanged by virtue of their townſmen and commiſſary, and without that virtue thouſands are loſt. I would entreat of my townſmen to take particular care of all priſoners taken, and ſend them on as ſoon as may be before we are all dead and loſt to the world. My ſituation don't admit me to expreſs myſelf as I ſhould be glad to do; and enlarging upon the ſubjeƈt dont avail anything. I am now in the limboes, in the midſt of filth and vermin."

Pennſylvania Packet, Thurſday Augᵗ. 30, 1781.

———

Extraƈt of a letter dated on board the priſon ſhip Jerſey, at New York, April 26, 1782.

" I am ſorry to write you from this miſerable place: I can aſſure you ſince I have been here we have had only twenty men exchanged, al

THE MARTYRS' VAULT.

though we are in number upwards of 700, ex-
clufive of the fick in the Hofpital fhips, who
died like fheep : therefore my intention is, if
poffible, to enter on board fome merchant or
tranfport fhip, as it is impoffible for fo many
men to keep alive in one veffel."

Pennfylvania Packet, Tuefday May 21, 1782.

---

*Extract of a letter dated on board the Jerfey (vul-
garly called Hell) Prifon Ship, New York, Auguft 10, 1781.*

There is nothing but death or entering into
the Britifh fervice before me. Our fhip's company is reduced to a fmall number (by death
and entering into the Britifh fervice) of 19.
There is a partial cartel arrived and bro't 11
prifoners, and the names of fo many as makes
up that number, fent from Bofton by fomebody,

and dam the villain that trades that way tho'
there is many fuch in that are making widows
and fatherlefs children a curfe on them all. The
commiffary told us, one and all to the number
of 400 men that the whole fault lays on Bofton,
and we might all be exchanged, but they never
cared about us; and he faid the Commiffaries
were damned rogues and liars.

"I am not able to give you even the outlines
of my exile; but thus much I will inform you that
we bury 6, 7, 8, 9, 10, and 11 men in a day: we
have 200 more fick and falling fick every day;
the ficknefs is the yellow fever, fmall pox, and
in fhort, everything elfe that can be mentioned.

"I had almoft forgot to tell you that our
morning's falutation is, "Rebels! turn out your
dead!"

Pennfylvania Packet, Tues. Sept. 4, 1781.

Salem, *December* 5.

A letter from an officer, late of a privateer from this port, dated on board the Jersey prison ship, New York, November 9th, says,

" The deplorable fituation I am in cannot ·be expreffed. The captains, lieutenants and failing mafters are gone to the provoft, but they have only got out of the frying pan into the fire. I am left here with about 700 miferable objects, eaten up with lice, and daily taking fevers, which carry them off faft."

Pennfylvania Packet, Thurfday Jan 2, 1783.

NOTES.

(1) WEST HARTFORD, or, as it was formerly called, *West Division*, is the western portion of Hartford township, on the west side of the Connecticut River, about 50 miles from its mouth. The City of Hartford occupies the Eastern portion on the river.

(2) We think it quite probable that Mr. G. was the *Lieutenant* Gillet, of Col. Huntington's Regiment, who with a number of other American officers captured at the Battle of Long Island, sent (Sept. 5, 1776) by flag for their baggage and cash. Their friends were requested to send next door to General Putnam's their trunks, &c., properly directed, and leave their cash at the General's, that they might be sent by the first flag. The Americans had not at this time evacuated the city.

5

(3) Authorities all feem to agree that as the laft boats were pufhing off from the Brooklyn fhore, the Britifh arrived within fight of the ferry, and opened a fire upon the retreating Americans, and compelled at leaft one to return. "3 or 4 men were miffing, who came off in a batteau." —*Independent (Bofton) Chronicle*, Sept. 19, 1776. "Three perfons who left the Ifland laft in a batteau, fell into the enemy's hands."—*N. E. Chronicle.* In a Britifh account of the retreat, it is faid, "We were in the rear of the enemy; fome were killed or taken prifoners in Brooklyn. We faw three or four boats afloat—fome boats not off. The *debris* of their rear guard embarked about 8 or 9 o'clock."—*Parliamentary Reg.*, Vol. 13.

(4) ARCHER.—In another account which we have from the family this gentleman is mentioned as one *Hutton.*

(5) HORSE NECK, is the name applied to Weft Greenwich, one of three parifhes into which the townfhip of Greenwich, Conn., is divided; and is derived from a peninfula on the Sound formerly ufed as a pafture for horfes. Putnam's Hill, located in Weft Greenwich, about five miles weft from Stamford, on the main road to New York, is cele-

brated as the fcene of General Putnam's wonderful exploit
of riding, on horfeback, down the fteep declivity, and thus
efcaping from the Britifh dragoons.

(6) JAMES DE LANCEY, of Weft Chefter County, New York,
Lt. Col. Commandant of a battalion of his uncle, the Senior
Oliver De Lancey. He was the fon of Peter De Lancey
and Elizabeth Colden, and was, for a confiderable time,
fheriff of Weft Chefter, in which, owing to his intimate
acquaintance with the country, he was ftationed feveral years
during the Revolution. His corps made free with the cattle
of that region, by which they earned the *foubriquet* of " Cow-
Boys," and, in 1777, he raifed and commanded a " crack"
company of light-horfe in his native county. The fame year
he was furprifed by one of Putnam's fcouting companies,
captured, and imprifoned at Hartford, Ct. In July, 1781,
he was again at Morrifania, and an abortive attempt was
made, by order of Wafhington, to capture or deftroy his
odious corps. At the peace, Col. De Lancey removed to
Nova Scotia, where, in 1794, he was appointed a member
of the Council ; and he died at Annapolis, in that Province,
in the year 1800.

(7) SUGAR-HOUSE.—In addition to the Provoſt Jail and
churches, ſeveral ſugar-houſes in the city were uſed for the confinement of American priſoners. The Liberty ſtreet Sugar-
Houſe, which is the more eminently hiſtorical one, and dif-
tinctly known as the " Old Sugar-Houſe," was the one in
which Mr. Gillet, and ſubſequently his ſon, was impriſoned.
It occupied the ſite now filled by Nos. 34 and 36 in that
ſtreet, and was a dark ſtone building, five ſtories in height,
with ſmall deep windows like port-holes, giving it the appearance of a priſon. Each ſtory was divided into two com-
partments. A large barred door opened on Liberty ſtreet,
and from another, on the ſoutheaſt ſide, a ſtair-caſe led to
gloomy cellars, which were uſed as dungeons. Around the
building was a narrow paſſage, in which the ſentinels conſtantly patrolled, and the whole was encloſed by a wooden
fence nine feet high.

(8) When, in January, 1852, Mr. Jacob Barker, of New
York, offered through the columns of the N. Y. Journal of
Commerce to preſent a cane made from the timber of the
Old Sugar-Houſe to the oldest ſurvivors of the Priſons of
New York, but four could be found, viz.: William Clark,
Salmon Moulton, Levi Hanford, and *Jonathan Gillet*.

(9) The HESSIANS were German foldiers, hired by the Britifh Government, of their mafters, the petty German princes, at fo much per head, to fight under the Britifh flag in America. They derived their name from the fact that the largeft portion was fupplied by the Landgrave of *Heſſe-Caſſel*. They were firft employed againſt the Americans in the memorable Battle of Long Iſland, Auguſt 27th, 1776. According to the terms agreed upon between their mafters and the Britifh Government, every Hanoverian foldier who fhould have ferved with the approbation of his fuperior officer, was to have a portion of ground not more than 50, nor lefs than 20 acres, rent free for ever. The expenfe of raifing a proper habitation, furnifhing fame, purchafing implements of hufbandry, &c., to be defrayed by the colony in which he fhall be then refident. The whole expenfe of recruiting to be provided for in like manner—viz.: 50 pounds for every foldier, and 100 for every trooper, rating his horfe at 50 and himfelf at as much more. They were to be ftationed and accommodated with barracks, firing, &c., at the expenfe of the feveral colonies in which they fhall happen to be quartered.

The following, though not exactly accurate, yet is the neareſt eſtimate we can make of the number of thefe troops furnifhed to Britain :

	No. of Troups.	Per-centage of population.	Loft.	Received Cafh.
Heffe Caffel	16,992	4.55	6,500	2,600,000
Brunfwick	5,723	3.45	3,015	780,000
Heffe Hanau	2,422	3.95	981	335,150
Anfpach	1,644	0.79	461	105,400
Waldeck	1,225	4.05	720	122,670
Anhalt	1,160	5.05	176	535,500
Total	29,166	3.64	11,853	£4,678,620
Hanover received	-		-	448,000
				£5,126,620

Many of the foldiers were kidnapped ftrangers, hence the above per-centage is not ftrictly accurate.

The enliftments became fo outrageous that the minifter of France, M. de Vibraye, made active reprefentations to feveral of the electoral princes, and ftated that if their fhameful enlift-ments of men continued, his Court would regard it as an act of hoftility, and would fufpend the fubfidies received, by thofe princes, of France.

Thefe odious practices of the Britifh Government were alfo condemned with indignation by Lord Chatham.

(10) GAGERS, evidently a miffpelling for *Yagers* or *Jagers*, who were a German corps commanded by Lt. Col. Wurmb. They were brought up to the ufe of the rifle-barrel gun in boar hunting, and were very expert in the ufe of that weapon.

In Germany they were employed, by the various petty princes, as forefters, and were allowed to take apprentices, whereby thefe markfmen became numerous. The Jagers came out here in 1776, and it is believed that about 1000 of them were employed, the Britifh Government fondly imagining that they would prove a complete match for the American rifle-men. Their uniform was green, faced with crimfon; the gun they ufed was a fmall rifle, and they fought in a fkulking manner, very much like our own Indians. Some of thefe Jager riflemen were in Arnold's expedition againft New Lon-don in 1781, where, in the attack on Fort Grifwold, they were reported to have exceeded all others in cruelty. At Fairfield, where they compofed the rear-guard, they fet fire to and deftroyed nearly everything which Gov. Tryon had fpared, including the large and elegant meeting-houfe, the minifters' houfes, Mr. Burr's and other dwellings, which had previoufly received the Governor's protection; tore his pro-tections in pieces, damned him roundly, and abufed females fhamefully—, finally moving off in a difgraceful manner. They proved themfelves the vileft banditti that figured in the Revolutionary War, and were emphatically " fons of plunder and devaftation." They were alfo engaged in the action at Spencer's Ordinary, June 26, 1781, at the Battle near Jamef-town Ifland, in the fame year, and elfewhere.

(11) Among "the feven" to whom Mr. Gillet refers as
having been taken with him, were Timothy Watfon, of Eaft
Windfor, Conn., and John Waterman; the latter was releafed from confinement in the prifon through the influence
of a brother Mafon, and was allowed the freedom of the city
on his parole. Perhaps, alfo, the *Roger Filer* and *John
Moody*, mentioned in the letter, may have belonged to the
fame party of unfortunates.

(12) So completely were the prifoners ftripped of clothing,
valuables, &c., that it is faid of the company confined with
Timothy Watfon, Mr. Gillet and others in the Old Sugar
Houfe, that *only fix* had decent clothes, and even thefe were
taken from the bodies of their companions who had died of
dyfentery and confinement.

(13) Impure air, water, and food, and the changes between the intenfe heat between decks by daytime, and the
chill dampnefs of night operating on the thinly clad and
half ftarved prifoners, were all fufficient caufes of dyfentery, or
"bloody flux," which raged among them with fearful vio-
lence. It was, indeed, *the* fcourge of the prifons and prifon-
fhips.

(14) " Houfes where once people attempted to implore
God's bleffings."—In addition to the jails and fugar houfes,
the following *churches* were converted into prifons for the
incarceration of victims of Britifh cruelty, viz.: the North
Dutch Church, yet ftanding, on William ftreet, between Fulton and Ann; the Middle Dutch Church, the prefent U. S.
Poft Office, which was ufed as a prifon for about two
months, and afterwards converted into a riding-fchool for
the Britifh cavalry; and the " Brick Church," which, until
within a few years, ftood in the triangle between Park Row,
Beekman and Naffau ftreets, was alfo ufed for a fhort time.
Subfequently this laft mentioned, together with the Prefbyterian Church in Wall ftreet, the Scotch Church in Cedar
ftreet, and the Friends' Meeting Houfe in Liberty ftreet,
were converted into hofpitals. The French Church in Pine
ftreet was ufed as a magazine for ordnance and ftores.

(15) " HUNTINGTON REGIMENT," fo named after its Colonel, JEDEDIAH HUNTINGTON, one of the five fons of Gen.
Jabes Huntington, who were all in the Continental army at
different times during the war. He was born at Norwich,
Conn., Aug. 15th, 1745, and graduated at Harvard College
in 1763, delivering, on that occafion, " the *firft Englifh* ora-

6

tion ever heard upon the commencement boards" of that inftitution. He early efpoufed the patriot caufe, was an active Son of Liberty, and one of the firft captains of the militia of his native State. In 1775 he raifed a regiment, with which he joined the Continental army, and, in 1778, received from Congrefs the commiffion of brigadier-general, which rank he held until the clofe of the war. In 1798 he was appointed Collector of the port of New London, by Wafhington, who entertained for him a high refpect, and there he refided until his death, on the 25th of September, 1818. By his firft marriage, he was allied to Gov. Trumbull, and his fecond wife was the daughter of Bifhop Moore, of Virginia. Of Col. Huntington's regiment were taken prifoners, *Captains*, Brewfter and Biffell ; *Lieutenants*, Makepeace, Orcutt, Gillet and Gay ; *Enfigns*, Lyman, Chapman, Hinman, Bradford, Higgins; *Adj.* Hopkins, *Dr.* Holmes, *Col.* Clark. In addition to thefe, there were reported as *miffing*, immediately after the battle, *fix* captains, *fix* lieutenants, *twenty-one* fergeants, *two* drummers, and 126 rank and file.

(16) Montozin Island, we confider to be a mifpronunciation and mifpelling of Montresor Island, (now Ran-

dall's Ifland, in the Eaft River) then fo called from its owner, Capt. Montrefor, an officer of the Britifh Engineers, who purchafed it in 1772, and lived upon it until the clofe of the Revolution. On the 24th of September, 1776, Colonel Jack-fon, with Major Henly (aid-de-camp to Gen. Heath) and 240 men, made a defcent upon the Britifh poft on this Island in flatboats, but were repulfed with a lofs of 22 men, among whom was Maj. Henly, who was fhot at the head of his men.

(17) STRATTON ISLAND, *i. e.*, Staten Island.

(18) FORT WASHINGTON, on the Eaft bank of the Hudfon, near New-York City, was captured by the Britifh on the 16th of November, 1776, and the garrifon of nearly 3000 men became prifoners of war.

(19) The children of Mr. Gillet were a fon, JONATHAN, whofe hiftory, fo fimilar in many refpects to the father's, has been before mentioned in this narrative; a fon ALMON, after-wards a hatter in Windfor, Conn.; a daughter, FLORA, who married Mr. Shem Stoughton; ESTHER, who married Mr. Samuel Terry; CORINNA, who is honored with a fpecial meffage in her father's prifon letter, and who married Mr. Ruf-fell Loomis, and was the mother of thirteen children; and a

fourth daughter, who married a Mr. Gibbs. Mr. Gillet's
widow (Elizabeth Steel, of West Hartford, to whom he was
married January 2, 1741) subsequently married Mr. Oliver
Stoughton, of East Windsor, Conn.

(20) EAST HARTFORD is a beautiful town on the east side of
the Connecticut river, opposite to the town of Hartford, on
the west side, within which it was formerly included, dating
its incorporation as a distinct town in 1784. It was for
many years distinguished, above any other town in the State,
for the variety and amount of its manufactures; in 1775, a
gunpowder mill was built there, under the special patronage
of the colony, which is believed to have been the first mill
of the kind erected in this country. In 1782, iron works
were built here, and in 1784, anchors, mill screws, nail rod,
paper, snuff, gunpowder, &c., were extensively manufactured
there.

(21) THE JERSEY, originally a sixty-four gun ship, having
been dismantled in 1776, on account of her unseaworthiness,
was placed in the Wallabout, off the Brooklyn shore, and
there used as a prison-ship till the close of the war, when
she was left to decay on the spot where her many victims
had suffered. Her character, as one of the most loathsome

and difmal prifons to which Britifh inhumanity configned their prifoners, is too well known, and has been too often recited to require any lengthy defcription at our hands. Sufficient it is to know that the terrible fufferings which were endured by thoufands of American foldiers and failors during the Revolutionary War, have rendered her name a fynonym for prifon-fhips.

(22) THE PERSEVERANCE. Probably the Britifh privateer brig of that name. She belonged to the port of New York, carried 16 guns, and was cruifing in May, 1782.

(23) NORWALK, Fairfield County, Conn., is between Darien and Weftport, on the Long Ifland Sound, being about 5 miles in length, and four in breadth. It was purchafed from the Indians as early as 1640, although fettlements were not commenced upon it until about 1649-50. On the 11th, of July, 1779, the village of Norwalk was burned by the Britifh and tories, under Gov. Tryon. "Old Well," now a flourifhing village, is fituated about 1½ miles fouth of the central part of Norwalk borough, on the west side of the creek, as Norwalk river is called at that point. Its name was derived probably from an *old well*, from which, in ancient times, vef-

fels engaged in the Weft India Trade, took their fupply of water.

(24) Capt. Seth Seymour was in command of a cavalry company during the Revolution, and a refident of the town of New Canaan, Conn., where he died.

Hanford enlifted in this troop in October, 1776.

(25) The names of this guard, with whom Hanford was captured, March 13, 1777, are as follows: Wright Everitt, Jona. Raymond, Samuel Huefted, Ebenezer Hoyt, James Hoyt, Jonathan Hillop, James Trowbridge, Matthew Com-ftock, Gideon St. John, ——— and 2 others under command of Lt. J. B. Eels.

(26) "OTHER HOSPITALS." See *note* 14.

(27) The "GOOD INTENT," on her voyage from England, was caft on the rocks at Halifax, and loft part of her keel, by which fhe was unfitted for fervice, and even while ufed as a prifon-fhip, fhe required the daily ufe of her pumps to keep her afloat.

(28) "OUR GOVERNOR," at this time, was Jonathan Trum-bull, of Connecticut.

(29) EBENEZER HOYT was a member of the fame company of cavalry with Levi Hanford, under the command of Capt. Seth Seymour. He was taken prifoner with Mr. Hanford, was confined with him in the Sugar Houfe, and they were the only furvivors of the party that was captured. They were liberated together, and returned home in company. After regaining his health, Mr. Hoyt again joined the company with Hanford, and continued in the performance of his duty to the end of the war. He died at an advanced age, where he had always lived, in the town of New Canaan, Conn.

(30) Probably Col. SETH HART, of the Connecticut troops.

ANTECHAMBER
TO THE
TOMB

ACCOUNT

OF THE

INTERMENT OF THE REMAINS

OF

AMERICAN PATRIOTS,

WHO PERISHED ON BOARD THE BRITISH PRISON SHIPS

DURING THE AMERICAN REVOLUTION.

WITH NOTES AND AN APPENDIX,

BY HENRY R. STILES, M. D.

NEW YORK:

PRIVATELY REPRINTED.

1865.

Edition 80 copies 8vo.
35 " 4to.

No.

PRESS OF J. M. BRADSTREET & SON.

AN

ACCOUNT

OF THE

INTERMENT OF THE REMAINS

OF

11,500

AMERICAN SEAMEN,

SOLDIERS AND CITIZENS,

WHO FELL VICTIMS TO THE CRUELTIES OF THE BRITISH,
ON BOARD THEIR PRISON SHIPS AT THE WALLABOUT,

During the

AMERICAN REVOLUTION.

With a Particular Defcription of the

GRAND & SOLEMN FUNERAL PROCESSION,

WHICH TOOK PLACE ON THE 26 MAY, 1808.

AND AN

ORATION,

Delivered at the

TOMB OF THE PATRIOTS,

BY BENJAMIN DE WITT, M. D.

A Member of the Tammany Society or Columbian Order.

———o———

Compiled by the

WALLABOUT COMMITTEE.

———o———

NEW-YORK:

PRINTED BY FRANK, WHITE, AND CO.

1808.

TO

ALDEN J. SPOONER, Esq.,

OF BROOKLYN,

THIS BOOK IS

RESPECTFULLY DEDICATED,

BY THE ANNOTATOR,

Not lefs as a tribute of perfonal efteem, than as a deferved recognition

OF HIS

EARNEST AND PERSISTENT EFFORTS, IN YEARS PAST,

TO SECURE FOR THE

REMAINS OF THE MARTYRS OF THE PRISON SHIPS

A

Befitting place of fepulture, and a noble monument,

IN THE CITY

Which has grown up around the fhores

OF THE

WALLABOUT.

January 1ft, 1865.

HISTORICAL ACCOUNT

OF THE

INTERMENT OF THE REMAINS

OF THE

American Martyrs

AT THE

WALLABOUT.

————•◆•————

 HE neglected fituation in which the relics of the American fea-men, foldiers, and citizens who were made prifoners by the Britifh, and perifhed on board their Prifon Ships during the Revolutionary War,

I

have been fuffered to remain, has long been a
fource of regret to the furvivors of that memorable conflict, and thofe of our countrymen who
rejoice in its glorious termination. The fentiment of grateful fympathy has not on this fubject
been limited or circumfcribed: it has been communicated to all clafses of citizens and all political parties. That thefe were the bones of
Americans, who fell in the caufe of their country,
was the confideration which produced an unanimous refolve to pay them the juft and only
tribute of affection that remained, a decent and
refpectful interment.

How, and under what circumftances, these
bones came to be depofited on the fhores and in
the fands of the Wallabout, is an enquiry, the
anfwer to which, if it were written with the pen
of that recording angel by whom are fet down all
the actions of the wicked and all the fufferings of
the good, would fwell this volume beyond the

bounds which are prefcribed to it, and might excite recollections and fenfations which would not be confined to this fide the Atlantic. Suffice it to ftate merely, that during the Revolution, the Britifh had ftationed at the Wallabout,[1] Long-Ifland, nearly oppofite the city of New-York, a number of Prifon Ships, on board of which it was the fate of thofe Americans, who had become prifoners of war, to be placed. The principal of thefe were the JERSEY, the remains of whofe hulk are ftill to be feen on the Long-Ifland fhore; the JOHN, the SCORPION, the STROMBOLO, and the HUNTER. From thefe floating dungeons, the hearts of whofe keepers muft indeed have delighted in the "luxury of woe," the bodies of our countrymen, having gone through the preparatory ftages of fuffering and death, were taken on fhore at the Wallabout, and thrown fcarcely beneath the furface.

" Each day at leaft fix carcafes we bore,

" And fcratch'd them graves along the fandy fhore.

" By feeble hands the fhallow graves were made,

" No stone memorial o'er the corpses laid.

" In barren fands, and far from home they lie,

" No friend to fhed a tear when paiiing by ;

" O'er the mean tombs infulting Britons tread,

" Spurn at the fand, and curfe the rebel dead."

Freneau's Poem.

The hafte and indignity with which they were committed to the earth were fuch, that many fkeletons have been difcovered in pofitions which clearly indicate and prove, that the graves, or holes, which were dug, were too confined to receive them at full length, and that, either from want of time or inclination to enlarge them, the bodies were crowded and prefsed down into the earth without decency or humanity.

How many perifhed on board thefe Prifon Ships, and how many were thus carried to this modern Golgotha, cannot be accurately ftated. It is afcertained, however, with as much precifion as the nature of the cafe will admit, that upwards of 11,000 died on board the JERSEY alone.[2] The probability therefore is, that the real number of victims were many thoufands more. The quantity of bones, which have withftood the ravages of time, and have been difcovered by digging away the ground for improvements in and adjacent to the navy-yard, is immenfe. Many have undoubtedly become fo mingled with their native duft, as not to be perceptible; and many will undoubtedly yet be found, as further advances in improving the ground are made.

Several cafks and boxes were filled with fuch as were collected by the workmen thus employed; and were preferved by John Jackfon,[3] efq., and others, for the purpofe of interment. Many patriotic individuals have for years paft urged the neceffity of a prompt attention to the difcharge of a duty fo important; all have acqui-

efced in the meafure; but it ftill remained un-
pcrformed. At length, in 1803, the Tammany
Society[*] took up the fubjeft, and agreed to the
following memorial, which was figned by feveral
mcmbers, and other citizens, and tranfmitted to
Congrefs :

MEMORIAL,

(*Prefented by* SAMUEL L. MITCHILL,[*] *Feb.* 10, 1803.)

To the Senate and Houfe of Reprefentatives of the United
States, in Congrefs aiTembled.

YOUR Memorialifts, citizens of the United
States, and inhabitants of the city of New-York,
beg leave to recall to the memory of your honourable body an event which you cannot but
have noticed; an event famous in hiftory, melancholy in its circumftances, and which, while it
awakens the tear of fympathy and regret, feems
alfo, in the opinion of your Memorialifts, to

claim fome attention from the political fathers of our country, the fupreme legiflature of the United States of America.

The lapfe of years is gradually drawing the veil of oblivion over the memories of thofe unfortunate men, our once efteemed fellow-citizens, who, when our country ftruggled for her rights and liberties, gallantly faced the moft powerful maritime nation of Europe on her own element, and were doomed, by the ill fortune of war, to languifh out their lives in extreme mifery and diftrefs on board the Prifon Ships of our enemies in the harbour of New-York.

It is perhaps unneceffary to remind your honourable body, that thoufands thus perifhed, who, animated by the divine fpirit of liberty, fuffered all the evils of imprifonment, exile, and want, rather than join the ftandard of *their* country's enemies ; and preferred death itfelf with all its horrors to the abandonment of *her caufe.* We cannot refuse our admiration to patriotifm fo pure and exalted!

Adjacent to the mooring-places of thefe float-ing prifons, where our brave feamen yielded their lives to the mercilefs policy, or native barbarity of a foreign foe, is the fite of the prefent navy-yard. In levelling the ground for its improve-ment, the earthly remains of thoufands of thefe gallant men have been, and ftill are daily feen, fcarce earthed in the falling banks, or expofed on the naked fhores. Thefe bones—thefe fkeletons —thefe relics of departed man, the hand of indi-vidual humanity has carefully collected for a decent interment, as the laft fad teftimony of regard and affection which can now be given to the memories of thofe men, whofe conftancy and patriotifm had endeared them to their country. The liberality of John Jackfon, efq., has induced the offer to appropriate an eligible piece of land, as the place of this folemn depofitory.

If the ancient Grecian Republics—if Athens, the nobleſt of them all—raiſed columns, temples, and pyramids to commemorate thoſe who fell in the fields of Marathon and Plateæ in defence of their country; can America be backward, and yet juſt, in paying her tribute of reſpect to the memories of citizens, who, equally patriotic and meritorious, periſhed leſs ſplendidly, in the priſ-ons of unheeded want and cruel peſtilence?

Without treſpaſſing further on the time of your honourable houſe, we would briefly ſuggeſt, that after preparing a decent tomb, where the precious relics of *theſe victims for the nation* may reſt undiſturbed and ſacred, until the Great Spirit has decreed the reſuſcitation of the dead, and the final conſummation of all things; we would wiſh to ſee erected ſome monument that may endure the rage of Time; neither lofty, nor ſumptuous, nor magnificent, but which may, neverthelefs, inform future ages, "Here lies the

2

remains of an immenfe multitude of men, who, preferring death to the facrifice of their honour and the fidelity they owed to their country, perifhed in the Prifon Ships at New-York."

If, in the eftimation of your honourable body, this be an object worthy of your attention, we would folicit fuch an appropriation toward the profecution of this defign, as your wifdom may deem requifite and juft.

New-York, January 31ft, 1803.

THE following is the anſwer of Dr. Mitchill to the Letter incloſing the Memorial :

Waſhington, February 10, 1803.

To Meſſrs. George J. Warner,
  William Mooney,[6]
  Nathan Sanford,[7]   *Committee of*
  William Boyd,[8]   *Tammany Society.*
  John Jackſon, and
  Edward Roberts,

Gentlemen,

I acknowledge the receipt of your affecting letter, dated January the thirty-firſt, and of the ſad memorial which accompanied it. My feelings were excited by the peruſal of theſe papers, as they brought to mind not only the mournful events of Britiſh Priſon Ships and cruelty, but renewed the ideas of thoſe human relics which I had ſurveyed ſeveral times laſt ſeaſon, on my viſits to the navy-yard.

This morning I offered your memorial to the House of Reprefentatives, and moved that it fhould be referred to the Committee of the whole Houfe, to which had been referred the bill from the Senate concerning monuments to be erected to the memory of Generals Woofter,[9] Herkimer,[10] Davidfon,[11] and Scriven. This was agreed to, and the memorial is accordingly thus difpofed of.

You may have read in the news-papers, that on the receipt of this bill from the Senate, a great number of monuments were propofed to be erected, to commemorate the revolutionary fervices of various brave officers who were flain in their country's caufe. All thefe were referred to a felect Committee for confideration. That Committee reported in favour of no more than four, additional to the four comprifed in the bill. Thefe are Warren,[12] Mercer,[13] Nafh[14] and De Kalb.[15] This report of amendments, together with the bill, ftands referred to that Committee of the whole Houfe, to which, on my motion this morning, your memorial, praying fome monumental appropriation for the wretched victims of the Prifon Ships, has alfo been referred.

As to the ultimate fuccefs of your patriotic application, Gentlemen, I dare not hold out to you any warm encouragement. For I think I difcern a difpofition among the majority in this Houfe to let the bill and amendments remain where they are, and do nothing more about them. Some are of opinion that Congrefs ought not to appropriate public money for fuch purpofes. Others think that the art of Printing has fuperceded the ufe and intention of monuments. Mention of your application will be recorded on the Journals of the Houfe of Reprefentatives, and be a lafting memorandum of your zeal and benevolence.

Be pleafed, Gentlemen, to communicate to the

brethren of Tammany Society, and the other subfcribers of the memorial, my prompt and refpectful attention to their wifhes, and to accept for yourfelves, and thofe whom you reprefent, the high expreffions of my regard.

SAMUEL L. MITCHILL.

From Congrefs much was expected, as the fubject of the application to them was purely national, and one which deeply interefted the public fenfibility. No meafures were, however, taken by that honourable body ; and the ftorms of feveral winters were permitted to vifit "too roughly" the unfheltered remains of the martyrs of American liberty.[18]

In the winter of 1807, the fubject was again brought forward in the Tammany Society, and a Committee (called the Wallabout Committee) appointed, to take meafures for carrying the long contemplated defign of interment into effect.

This Committee, on the firſt of February, 1808, preſented the following report to the Society, which was accepted and confirmed, and ordered to be recorded on the minutes:

The Committee appointed by the Tammany Society or Columbian Order to make arrangements reſpecting the interment of the relics of American Seamen, Soldiers, and Citizens at the Wallabout,

REPORT,

That the taſk committed to them is one of a nature the moſt ſolemn and impreſſive. The ſufferings of our unfortunate countrymen on board the Jerſey, and other Priſon Ships, is a theme on which the imaginations of the ſurvivors will never ceaſe to dwell, and to which the commiſerating eye of humanity will never ceaſe to advert. The ſevere yet humble, the intolerable yet obſcure fate of thoſe victims to the cruelty of their and their country's oppreffors fhall not be unrecorded, but fhall be ftamped on our memories and engraven on every heart that beats with the blood or glows with the fentiments of a citizen, of a fon of America. Shall it be told, fhall it be proclaimed to the world, that while other nations celebrate the heroifm and the virtues of thofe who have diftinguifhed themfelves on great and interefting occafions, and with the zeal of enthufiafm and the fervency of religion, preferve and perpetuate their memory and em balm the bodies rendered facred and venerable by the actions they performed; the American people, more enlightened in their views, more exalted in their ftations, and more dignified in their native character, can at once forfeit all claim to their diftinguifhed pre-eminence, and fink infinitely beneath the darknefs and barbarity of ages that are paft, by the practice of that moft odious of vices and worft of crimes—Ingratitude! Ingratitude to the memory of thofe who fuffered, who bled, who died in their caufe! who bore the tauntings of reproach, the lafh of vengeance, and drank to its very dregs the cup of mifery, rather than permit their quivering lips or their fainting breath to violate or profane their country's name or honour: whilft the excruciating tortures to which they were fubjected, might have wrung the hearts of the mercenary hirelings of Great Britain, the prefence of fome of whom ftill encumbers the American foil, and fills every beholder with involuntary fhuddering;—whofe magnanimity in fuffering might have taught an inftructive leffon to a Howe, a Burgoyne, or a Cornwallis, and will emulate the examples of Grecian or Roman ftory; whofe crime was love of liberty; whofe lives were given up on her altar.

Yet this part of our hiftory can fcarcely be told, fince the tale which it reveals is connected

3

with the fhame of our countrymen, and with every incident which it unfolds, records a correfponding mark of their difgrace.

Painful as it is, fuch is the melancholy fact. The American name has been tarnifhed, and the American Eagle, while foaring through the vaft expanfe, has been arrefted in his courfe, as he has looked down from the commanding heights he had gained to his favourite fpot, and obferved this foul, this indelible ftain upon our reputation.

Nearly five-and-twenty years have now paffed away fince the clofe of the revolutionary conteft. According to the eftablifhed laws of honourable warfare, contending armies, though ftill panting for victory and thirfting for each others' blood, will confent to a temporary fufpenfion of arms for the purpofe of allowing the mutual though melancholy fatisfaction of obeying the firft impulfe of nature, and burying their refpective dead. Yet, at the clofe of fo long a period, we find the bones of our country's brave defenders ftill bleaching beneath the winter's ftorm and the fummer's fcorching fun, and whitening the fields which were once encrimfoned with their blood; as if to throw a mantle over the neglect which deprives them of a fhelter, and which might rife up in judgment againft our hands, which ftill continue to commit it. And efpecially it appears to your Committee, that that portion of the relics of our countrymen who perifhed on board the Jerfey Prifon Ship, in which inhuman tortures were inflicted with infernal ingenuity and malignity, and which literally deferved the name it fometimes received, are entitled to the peculiar regard and attention of the friends to the caufe in which they fuffered: more particularly at this period, when our peace is about to be interrupted, and fome of us may fhortly be called upon to avenge or fhare their fate.

Your committee, therefore, feeling anxious
that no time fhould be loft, beg leave to report
in part, and refpectfully to recommend :

1ft, That the Tammany Society, or Columbian Order, from their national ftructure and organization, being entitled to originate meafures
on this fubject, do immediately proceed to the
adoption of a plan for the purpofe of interring
with fuitable rites and ceremonies the bones of
our countrymen who perifhed on board the Jerfey Prifon Ship, now lying on the fhores of the
Wallabout.

2nd, That, as a part of this plan, a circular
letter be prepared, containing a general invitation, as well to the friends and relations of thofe
unfortunate perfons, as to our fellow-citizens at
large, to forward fuch information as may be in
their poffeffion, or knowledge of the names,
places of birth, age, rank and families of thofe
perfons, either to the Grand Sachem, brother

John Jackfon, or the Chairman of this Committee. This circular to be publifhed by fuch
of the editors of newfpapers in the United States
as may think proper to infert it, and to be fent
to fuch perfons as may be likely to afford particular information.

3rd, That the different patriotic Societies' and
public bodies be invited to join in the arrangements, and to appoint committees to confer with
the Committee of Tammany Society. And particularly that the reverend the clergy, and all
the Public Officers, Military and Civil, of the
town of Brooklyn, the Corporation of the city of
New-York, the different Military Corps, and all
Officers of diftinction that can conveniently be
affembled, together with the citizens at large, be
requefted to unite on the occafion.

4th, The Committee do particularly recommend, that an Orator be felected by the Society,
for the purpofe of addreffing the affemblage which

will be collected : the Society not to be confined
in their choice to a member of their body.

5th, That a monument, of American materials
and workmanſhip, be erected, with ſuitable inſcriptions, emblematical in its deſign and execution, and deſcriptive of the events we are about
to commemorate.

6th, That meaſures be immediately taken for
defraying the expences incident to this ſerious
and important undertaking.

All which is ſubmitted to the Society.

Jacob Vandervoort,[17]
John Jackſon,
Iſſachar Cozzens,[18]
Burdet Stryker,[19]
Robert Townſend, junr.[20]
Benjamin Watſon,[21]
Samuel Cowdrey,[22]

*Wallabout Com-
mittee.*

New-York, February 1, 1808.

The Committee alſo iſſued the following Circular Letter, which it was requeſted by them ſhould be publiſhed in the different papers throughout the United States, and a copy of which was ſent by them to thoſe public Societies and public and revolutionary characters of which they could gain information :

CIRCULAR.

New-York, February 11, 1808.

THE Committee appointed by the Tammany Society, or Columbian Order, of the city of New-York, to make arrangements reſpecting the Interment of the Relics of American Seamen, Soldiers, and Citizens who periſhed on board the JERSEY[22] Priſon Ship during the Revolutionary War, now lying on the ſhores of the Wallabout, (Long-Iſland) beg leave to ſubmit the ſubject of their appointment to the conſideration of the ſurviving relatives and friends of thoſe unfortunate perſons in every part of the United States, and of their enlightened and patriotic fellow-citizens at large.

Various attempts have been made to accomplifh this important and interefting object. But individual exertions have hitherto proved incompetent; and the public fenfibility, too much occupied by other confiderations, has not as yet been fufficiently excited by the appeals that have been made to it.

This indifference, fo prevalent to the memory of thofe of our country's brave defenders, who fell victims to the unrelenting cruelty of her enemies, while it muft fill every ingenuous mind with regret, is calculated to fix upon the American nation a charge, which, while they abhor, they provoke and juftify by their conduct.

Perhaps, in the hiftory of nations, there is no trait of human nature more ftrongly and clearly delineated, than the impaffioned and devout regard which is entertained and exhibited by the furvivors of glorious and warlike enterprizes, towards the memory of their companions in arms, who, being engaged in the fame conflicts, fharing the fame dangers, animated by the fame love of country, and achieving the fame victory, or fuftaining the fame defeat with themfelves, have found an honourable grave. In fome countries, their bodies have been embalmed; in others, monuments have been erected in commemoration of their heroic conftancy and valour, and their contempt of death: And in all, the memory of their deeds has been perpetuated, their names have been enrolled in the faithful volume of hiftory, and handed down to pofterity, and they ftill live in their virtuous examples and the immortality of their fame.

Shall America furnifh an exception to a cuftom fo firmly eftablifhed, fo rational, fo meritorious? Shall it be faid—Americans have already for-gotten their flaughtered countrymen; that, as

4

they behold the earth still strewed with their bones, they can pass calmly and indifferently by, and refuse them the " tribute of a sigh" and the common rights of interment ; and that, while in the full enjoyment of Independence, they can shew the most unfeeling neglect to the toil, the treasure, and the blood of which it is the purchase ?

The society by which this committee is appointed are encouraged to think that such will not be the case. But that their exertions to rescue from oblivion, and place on an imperishable basis, the memory of a large portion of those who perished in the revolutionary contest, will meet with suitable countenance and support.

They have long indulged the hope, that others to whom the task, with equal, if not greater propriety, belonged, would undertake its execution. They have been anxious to avoid the appearance of an ostentatious display before the public, and would cheerfully have lent their humble aid to any meafures which the general or their ftate government might have adopted on the occafion. Being difappointed in their wifhes, and confidering that the firft and greateft objeɛt of their inftitution is the promotion of the interefts, the welfare, and the honour of their country, they have at length refolved to originate meafures on this fubjeɛt.

They have accordingly appointed this Committee, and invefted them with powers to form a plan for the Interment of that portion of the remains of our countrymen now lying on the fhores of Long Ifland. The Committee have procured from John Jackfon, efq., on whofe farm they were depofited, and where they now lie, a Deed of a piece of ground, confpicuoufly and advantageoufly fituated, being near the head of the navy-yard, and which will not be affeɛted by any regulations that may hereafter take place. He has already planted fome trees of an appropriate defcription on the fpot felected, and given to the Society permiffion to inter the bones in fuch manner and with fuch folemnities as they may think proper.

It is confidered by the Society that no further delay ought to take place. They have accordingly fanctioned the plan reported to them, which it is intended fhall be carried into execution as foon as the feafon will admit.

In the meantime the relatives and friends of thofe unfortunate perfons, and alfo our fellow-citizens at large, are requefted to forward immediately, either to Benjamin Romaine, efqr., Grand Sachem of Tammany Society, John Jackfon, efqr., or the Chairman of this Committee, by mail, or other fafe conveyance, fuch information as may be in their poffeffion or knowledge of the Names, Places of Birth, Age, Rank and Families of thofe perfons; together with fuch circumftances refpecting each as may be intereft-

ing, and particularly fuch as relate to their fituation and fufferings on board the faid fhip. This
information is indifpenfably neceffary, as it is
contemplated to erect a Monument, emblematical in its defign and execution, and defcriptive
of the events about to be commemorated. It is
alfo important in an hiftorical point of view, and
will be ufeful to the prefent generation and to
pofterity.

A proceffion will take place, compofed of different Societies, Public Bodies, and the Citizens
at large, and Military honours will be paid on
the occafion.—An Eulogium will be delivered to
the affemblage by a fuitable character, due notice
of which will be given to the public.

As it is defirable that the monument contemplated to be erected, fhould exhibit a finifhed
fpecimen of American tafte and patriotifm, and
will confequently be expenfive in its materials
and workmanfhip, fuch perfons as may be de-

firous of having the names of their relatives or
friends who are intended to be commemorated,
engraved upon it, and thofe who may have it in
their power, and feel defirous to promote this
undertaking, are requefted to forward their con-
tributions to either of the three perfons before
mentioned, or to authorife fome perfon in the
city of New-York to fubfcribe for the purpofe
in their behalf. The amount of this expence it
is eftimated need not exceed ten thoufand dollars.

The Committee entertain a confidence that
this invitation will meet with the approbation
and compliance of every friend to the caufe in
which many fell a facrifice, and many who ftill
furvive, fuffered and bled.

By order of the Committee,

JACOB VAN DERVOORT, *Chairman.*

Robert Townfend, junr. Secretary.

The Committee received the following com-
munications, which are felected from a variety of
others, all expreffing the fame approbation of the
undertaking:

Fort Columbus,[24] March 4, 1808.
Gentlemen,

I have the honour of acknowledging the receipt of your letter of the 24th February, together with a copy of your Society's Circular
Letter of the 11th ult., and after mature confideration, beg leave to exprefs my opinion of your
Refolutions. I confider them laudable, humane,
and calculated to reflect honour, not only on the
Society who promulgated the defign, but on the
country at large.

I have therefore opened a fubfcription at this
Garrifon for the purpofe of contributing as much
as poffible towards carrying your praifeworthy
views into effect.

It is with pleafure I inform you that the majority of the officers and foldiers under my command cheerfully entered into the fubfcription as liberally as circumftances would permit.

Enclofed you will find one hundred and fifty dollars, the amount of the contribution, the receipt of which you will pleafe to acknowledge.

I have the honour to be, very refpectfully,

Gentlemen,

Your obedient,

Humble fervant,

R. C. WHILEY.

Capt. Art. Com.

Robert Townfend, junr.
Secretary of the Committee of
Tammany Society.

New-York, March 5, 1808.

Sir,

Yesterday the Republican Green Rifle Corps paraded to celebrate the seventh anniversary of Mr. Jefferson's elevation to the Presidency. The different evolutions having been gone through, a hollow square was formed, and the letter read which I had the honour of receiving from you. The corps unanimously approved of the sentiments it contained, as laudable and patriotic, reflecting inextinguishable lustre on your Society, and cancelling for the Republic the debt of gratitude for benefits which ought never to be forgotten.

As private *Citizens* the corps have already contributed liberally to the pecuniary object of your letter; and as *Soldiers* they will heartily cooperate in any arrangement that may be made for rendering military honours to the remains of

thofe citizens who were bafely immolated by the
minions of a perfecuting and tyrannical government.

I remain with refpect, Sir,

Your moft obedient fervant,

FRANCIS M'CLURE,

Commandant Republican Greens.

Robert Townfend, junr.

Secretary to the Committee of
Tammany Society.

New-York, April 5, 1808.

Sir,

At a meeting of Capt. Henry Morgan's[n] Company of the 3d Regiment of Artillery, held laft
evening, your communication, by order and in
behalf of the Committee of Tammany Society,
together with the Circular iffued by them, refpecting the Interment of the Relics of American
Seamen, Soldiers, and Citizens, who perifhed on

board the Jerfey Prifon Ship at the Wallabout, during the Revolutionary War, was laid before the faid company, and we, being a Committee appointed out of the faid Company, are author-ifed to ftate, that they freely concur in the meafures that have been adopted for carrying the fame into effect. With fentiments of due refpect, we have the honour to be, Sir,

Your moft obedient and humble fervants,

By order and in behalf of the Company,

James Benedict,
Nathaniel I. Hubbard, } *Committee.*
Andrew Hegeman,[29]

Robert Townfend, junr.
Secretary of Wallabout Committee.

TO THE WALLABOUT COMMITTEE.

Gentlemen,

I had the honour of receiving your letter of the 24th of February, together with the Circular

which it enclofed. They were both communicated to the Society at their meeting ; and I have
the fatisfaction to inform you, Gentlemen, that
the fubject of them met their entire approbation
and concurrence ; they confider your proceedings
as reflecting the higheft honour not only on the
Committee, but likewife on the Society that appointed them, and will cheerfully lend their
feeble affiftance toward carrying your laudable
intentions into effect.

In behalf of the Hatter's Society,

J. HALSTED.

March 5, 1808.

New York, March 5, 1808.

Sir,

Agreeable to your requeft I laid your communication before the Company under my command, and am happy to inform you that they

approved of the meafure fpecified in it unanimoufly.

John Minuse, Capt.[*]

Robert Townfend, junr.
  Secretary of Committee of
  Tammany Society.

New-York, March 6, 1808.

Sir,

The letter of the Secretary of the Committee
of Tammany Society, enclofing their Circular of
the 11th ult., directed to the Prefident of the
Hibernian Provident Society, has been laid before that body at their laft meeting, and the
objeƈt of that communication highly approved of
by them.

I have it in command to inform you, that the
Hibernian Provident Society will cheerfully co-
operate with the Sons of Tammany in paying the
contemplated (and fo long negleƈted) refpeƈt to

the memory of the Martyrs of our Revolution, as well as on all occafions that may tend to elevate the charaćter and promote the welfare of our common country.

By order of the Hibernian Provident Society,

IGNS. REDMOND, Sect.[28]

To the Prefident of the
Tammany Society.

New-York, March 12, 1808.

Mr. Robert Townfend, junr.

Sir,

Your letter of the 24th ult., enclofing a Circular in relation to the Interment of the remains of our countrymen at the Wallabout, was duly fubmitted to the Cooper's Society, and agreeably to their wifhes I tranfmit you an anfwer.

They unanimoufly concur in the fteps taken by your Committee for carrying into effećt the objećt they have in view, and will cordially join

(41)

in fuch meafures as may be hereafter adopted by
your Society, for the purpofe of paying a refpectful tribute to the remains of our countrymen who
died in the caufe of liberty.

   By order of the Cooper's Society,

     John Walker, Sect.[20]

Sir,

I have the honour to acknowledge the receipt
of your note, written on the part of the Committee of Tammany Society, and covering their
Circular. Permit me, in reply, to exprefs my
wifhes for the fuccefs of an undertaking fo honourable to the Society who have originated it,
and fo interefting to the feelings of every American. I truft that through their attentions the
remains of our unfortunate countrymen will at
length receive the rites of fepulture, and their
memories the tribute of a monument.

I regret that the fubordinate nature of my

military command will not enable me to yield that
material co-operation in the funeral folemnities
which the Committee appear to defire.   I fhall,
however, be happy to render any affiftance in my
power.

I am, with refpect,

Your moft obedient fervant,

P. IRVING.[30]

Robert Townfend junr., Efq.
Secretary of Tammanial Committee.

New York, March 14, 1808.
Mr. Robert Townfend, junr.

Sir,

I have to inform you that the General Society
of Mechanics and Tradesmen of the City of
New-York,[31] unanimoufly concur in the honours
intended to be paid the remains of American
Soldiers, Seamen, and Citizens, who perifhed on
board the Jerfey and other Britifh Prifon Ships

during our Revolutionary War; and have appointed the following perfons a Committee to
confer with fuch others as may be appointed from
the different public bodies to make the neceffary
arrangements.

Cornelius Crygier,[32]
Anthony Steenback,[33]
James W. Lent,[34]
Thomas Mercein,[36]
John J. Labagh.[36]

JAMES HOPSON, Sect.[37]

Houfe Reprefentatives, U. S. March 21, 1808.
Sir,

I had the honour to receive your favour,
under date of the 10th inft. together with a copy
of the Circular Letter from the Committee of
the Tammany Society of New-York, of which
you are Secretary. The perufal of that letter has
brought to mind the mournful events connected

with the hiftory of Britifh Prifon Ships, thofe receptacles of human woe. Your refolutions are viewed here as praife-worthy, laudable, humane, and reflect the higheft honour on our country, and on your Society in particular.

I beg you will have the goodnefs to communicate to the Tammany Society my refpectful attention to their requeft, and accept for yourfelf, and thofe whom you reprefent, the efteem with which I have the honour to be, Sir,

> Your moft obedient humble fervant,
>
> GURDON S. MUMFORD.[38]

Robert Townfend, junr. Efq.

Secretary of the Committee of

Tammany Society.

New-York, March 22, 1808.

TO THE COMMITTEE OF THE TAMMANY SOCIETY.

Gentlemen,

Having been one of thofe American Seamen

who was confined on board the Jerfey Prifon
Ship during our ftruggle for independence, I had
an opportunity of witnefling the unexampled fufferings of my intrepid countrymen and brother
feamen: and though I confefs that it will be
impoffible for me to pourtray our fufferings in fo
animated, eloquent, and pathetic a manner as the
fubject juftly demands, yet I beg that your Society will indulge me, and pay attention to my
narrative. They will be pleafed to recollect, that
out of forty-three years that I have lived in the
world, more than thirty of them have been employed on the ocean in moft parts of the world.
I have therefore found but little leifure to
improve and cultivate even the very limited
facultics with which, by nature, I have been en-
dowed. You will however, I prefume, agree
with me, that a plain, fimple ftatement of facts
will carry conviction to every mind.

The firft time that I was on board the Jerfey

Prifon Ship was in 1782. I was taken in a letter of marque from Baltimore, bound for the Havana, by the Britifh King's frigate Ceres, on board of which fhip we were treated in a moft fhameful and barbarous manner by her commander. From that fhip we were, at fea, put on board the Champion twenty-four gun fhip, and brought into this port, and from her fent on board the Jerfey Prifon Ship, where I found about 1,100 American prifoners; amongft them feveral of my own townsmen, and all the prifoners in the moft deplorable situation.

I foon found that every fpark of humanity had fled the breafts of the Britifh officers who had charge of that floating receptacle of human mifery; and that nothing but abufe and infult was to be expected; for the mildeft language made ufe of to the prifoners was, *You damn'd yankee;* and the moft common, *You damn'd rebellious yankee rafcals.* This language at length became fo familiar to our ears, however infulting it was at firſt, that we took no more notice of it than we did of the whiſtling of the wind paſſing over our heads. Many of the priſoners, during the feverity of winter, had ſcarcely clothes ſufficient to cover their nakedness, and but very few enough to keep them warm: to remedy thoſe inconveniencies we were obliged to keep below, and either get into our hammocks or keep in conſtant motion, without which precautions we muſt have periſhed. But, to cap the climax of infamy, we were fed (if fed it might be called) with proviſions not fit for any human being to make uſe of: putrid beef and pork and worm-eaten bread, condemned on board their ſhips of war, was ſent on board the Jerſey to feed the priſoners: water, ſent from this city in a ſchooner called (emphatically called) the Relief!—water which, I affirm, without the fear of refutation, was worſe than I ever had, or ever ſaw, on a three years' voyage to the Eaſt

Indies: water, the scent of which would have dif-
compofed the olfactory nerves of a Hottentot;
while within a cable's length of the fhip, on
Long-Ifland, there was running before our eyes,
as though intended to tantalize us, as fine, pure,
and wholefome water as any man would wifh to
drink. The queftion will very naturally be afk-
ed, Why, if good water was fo near at hand, it
was not procured for us, inftead of bringing it at
confiderable expenfe and trouble from the city?
It is impoffible for any one, but thofe who had
the direction of the bufinefs, to anfwer that queftion fatisfactorily; but the object in bringing the
water from New York was to me, and the reft of
the prifoners, as felf-evident as the plain and fimple fact that two and two make four: becaufe the
effects that water had on the prifoners could not
be concealed, and were a damning proof why it
was filled in New York. On the upper gun deck
of the Jerfey, hogs were kept in pens by thofe

officers who had charge of her for their own ufe;
they were fometimes fed with bran; the prifoners,
whenever they could get an opportunity undif-
covered by the fentries, would, with their tin pots,
fcoop the bran from the troughs, and eat it, (after
boiling, when there was fire in the galley, which
was not always the cafe,) with feemingly as good
an appetite as the hogs themfelves.

The fecond and laft time I was on board the
Prifon Ship, was in February and March, 1783,
juft before peace took place. I was taken in a
brig from Providence, (R. I.) off the Capes of
Virginia, by the Fair American privateer of this
port, commanded and officer'd principally with
refugees; though it is doing Capt. Burton but
bare juftice to declare, that he treated us civilly,
and with much more humanity than I had before
experienced from Hawkins, commander of the
Britifh king's fhip Ceres, whofe inveterate hatred
of Americans was never exceeded by any man

living. The only hard treatment on board the
Fair American was being kept in irons the whole
time: but that was a precautionary meafure on
the part of her commander; there being fo many
prifoners on board, who doubtlefs would have
availed themfelves of any opportunity that might
have offered to have rifen upon the privateer.
We were brought within the Hook by her, and
fent up to the city in a pilot-boat. We had our '
irons knocked off at the Crane-wharf, and from
thence we were fent on board the Jerfey, in the
fchooner Relief, before mentioned. On my arrival again on board the Jerfey, which I had left
but a few months before, I found more prifoners
than I had left, though but very few of my former fellow-prifoners: fome of them had got
away, but the greater part had paid the debt of
nature, and their bones, with others, are the objects of your prefent folicitude and patriotic exertions.

There being fo many prifoners on board the
Jerfey, and others daily arriving, two or three
hundred of us were fent on board the John tranfport, which they had converted into a Prifon
Ship, and where the treatment we received was
much worfe than on board the Jerfey. We were
fubjected to every infult, every injury, and every
abufe that the fertile genius of the Britifh officers
could invent and inflict. For more than a
month we were obliged to eat our fcanty allowance, bad as it was, without cooking, as no fire
was allowed us; and I verily believe that it was
the means of haftening many out of exiftence.
One circumftance I think deferves particular
notice, as it was a moft fingular one:—A young
man of the name of Bird, a native of Bofton or
its neighbourhood, was one evening, with others,
playing at cards to pafs away the time. At about
ten o'clock I retired with my coufin to our hammock; we had but juft got afleep when we were

called by one of the card party, who requefted us to turn out, for that Bird was dying: we did turn out, and went to where he lay, and found him in the agonies of death; and in about fifteen or twenty minutes he was a corpfe. It was mentioned to the fentry at the gangway that one of the prifoners was dead, and the body was foon hurried on deck. The impreffion Bird's death made on our minds is ftill frefh in my recollection: that he was poifoned we had no doubt, as his body had fwelled very confiderably, and two hours before he was, to all appearance, as well as any of us. Many, fhortly after, went off in the fame manner, and amongft them my coufin, Oliver C. Coffin. I did but juft efcape the fame fate: I was taken ill before I left the Prifon Ship, and my legs began to fwell; but being exchanged, or rather being bought off, I made out to reach my father's houfe in a moft deplorable fituation. I was attended in my ficknefs by a

noted tory phyfician, Dr. Tupper, who declared
to my mother, that nothing could have faved my
life but having, as he expreffed himfelf, a conftitution of iron; for that he knew of nothing that
could have affected me in the manner in which I
was affected but poifon of fome kind or other.
Is it poffible then, after all thefe facts, for any
perfon to form any other opinion than that there
was a premeditated, organized fyftem purfued to
deftroy men whom they dare not meet openly
and manfully as enemies, in that bafe, inhuman,
and cowardly manner. It is an old adage, and a
very true one, that the brave are generous, and
the coward favage and cruel; and it was never
more completely exemplified than in the conduct
of the Britifh officers in this country during the
Revolution. Their cruelties here, and in India,
have become proverbial. Let it not be faid in
extenuation, that thofe cruel deeds were neceffary
to reprefs the fpirit of revolt, for every man of

common fenſe knows that cruelties exerciſed towards revolters, unleſs they can be completely
ſubdued, only tend to irritate and urge them on
to a more determined and deſperate reſiſtance.
We acknowledge we were revolters, but our revolt was legitimate; we revolted againſt oppreſ-
ſion, againſt a government that had revolted (if
I may be allowed the expreſſion) againſt its own
ſubjects, and violated the moſt ſacred of all duties
towards its people—the duty of defending and
protecting their conſtitutional rights and privileges, which had been left them as a legacy by
their brave anceſtors, who had fought and bled
to obtain them, in common with Engliſhmen.

There are other facts which perhaps are not
generally known to the American people, that I
ſhall mention.—One is, that a man of the name
of Gavot, a native of Rhode-Iſland, died, as was
ſuppoſed, and was ſewed up in his hammock,
and in the evening carried upon deck to be taken

with others who were dead, and thofe who might
die during the night, on fhore to be interred, (*in
their mode of interring.*) During the night it
rained pretty hard : in the morning, when they
were loading the boat with the dead, one hammock was obferved by one of the Englifh feamen
to move ; he fpoke to the officer, and told him
that he believed the man in that hammock
(pointing to it) was not dead. *In with him,* faid
the officer; *if he is not dead, he foon will be :* but
the honeft tar, more humane than his officer,
fwore he never would bury a man alive, and
with his knife ripped open the hammock, when,
behold—the man was really alive. What was
the caufe of this man's reanimation, is a queftion
for doctors to decide : it was at the time fuppofed, that the rain during the night had caufed
the reaction of the animal functions, which were
fufpended, but not totally annihilated. This
fame man, Gavot, went afterwards in the fame

flag with me to Rhode-Iſland. Capt. Shubael
Worth, of Hudſon, was maſter of the flag, and
will bear teſtimony to the ſame fact.

Another fact is, that although there were ſeldom leſs that 1000 priſoners conſtantly on board
the Jerſey, new ones coming about as faſt as the
old ones died, and were exchanged, (which by the
bye was but ſeldom,) I never, in the two different times that I was on board, knew of but one
priſoner entering on board a Britiſh ſhip of war,
though the boats from the fleet were frequently
there, and the Engliſh officers were endeavouring
to perſuade them to enter; but their perſuaſions
and offers were invariably treated with contempt,
and even by men who pretty well knew they
ſhould die where they were. Theſe were the men
whoſe bones have ſo long been bleaching on the
ſhores of the Wallabout; thoſe were the patriots
who preferred death in its moſt horrible ſhape to
the diſgrace and infamy of fighting the battles of

a bafe and barbarous enemy, againft the liberties of their country ; thofe were the patriots whofe fame fuffers no diminution by a comparifon with the heroes and patriots of antiquity! Shall Americans, then—fhall we, the furvivors of that glorious Revolution—refufe the humble tribute of refpect and veneration due to the memories of thofe heroes, and the common rights of fepulture to all that remains of them that is mortal? Forbid it Heaven! Let it not be faid that Americans are ungrateful, that they have received a legacy, and that the heroes who loft their lives in affifting to obtain it, becaufe dead, are not to be remembered.

I am aware that by what I have faid I fhall incur the difpleafure of fome with whom I have been on terms of intimacy—be it fo ; I court not the favours of the enemies of my country, nor do I fear their frowns. I am an American ; have fought for and fuffered in the caufe of my country, and but few, if any, have fuffered by the Britifh more than I have.

I have now, Gentlemen, given as correct a ftatement of facts, relative to our treatment on board the Prifon Ships by the Britifh, during our Revolutionary War, as I can from memory, after fuch a lapfe of time; and I feel confident that I have added nothing but what came immediately within my own knowledge and experience: and I affure you that I felt pleafed when I faw your advertifement in the papers, ftating your determination to pay the tribute due to the memories of thofe brave but unfortunate men; and their furviving relatives and friends will acknowledge the obligations they are under to you, and to John Jackfon, efq., for your fteady perfeverance in fo humane and laudable an undertaking. Though a monument fhould not be raifed by the hands of men to commemorate their fufferings and virtues, there is in the breaft of every true American an indelible monument of them which never will be effaced fo long as the blood continues to circulate through their veins. Although your Society has been defamed for the lead they have taken in the bufinefs, you will remember that it is by thofe who never fuffered, and who perhaps would not be difpleafed to fee the fame tragedy again acting on the fame Theatre, by the fame actors.

I now, after wifhing you every fuccefs in your prefent undertaking, conclude, and beg you to accept the affurance of my refpect and efteem.

ALEXANDER COFFIN, junr.

In Common Council, March 28, 1808.

The Committee, to whom was referred the communication enclofing a Circular Letter iffued by the Tammany Society, refpecting the interment of the relics of American Seamen, Soldiers, and Citizens, who perifhed on board the Jerfey

8

Prifon Ship, at the Wallabout, during the Revolutionary War, report,

That they have taken the fubject of that communication into confideration, and while it brings
to recollection an event which muft awaken the
fenfibility of every American Citizen, ftill it
feems to have been referved for the Tammany
Society alone to have originated meafures for
refcuing from oblivion, and placing on an imper-
ifhable bafis, the memory of a large portion of
our unfortunate, but much lamented fellow-citizens, who perifhed defending the precious rights
of our liberty and independence.

Your committee are therefore of opinion, that
the interment of the bones of our unfortunate
countrymen in the manner as propofed, will be
the means of tranfmitting to pofterity an event,
which will be deeply engraven on the heart of
every American.

Feeling, on an occafion of this nature, the importance of this communication, they do highly approve of the laudable and patriotic meafures adopted by the Tammany Society, and do recommend, that we give to an undertaking of this nature every encouragement that may be confistent with the duties of the Common Council.

Your Committee therefore further recommend, that the following refolutions may be adopted :

Refolved, That the Common Council do highly approve of the patriotic meafures taken by the Tammany Society, or Columbian Order, for interring the remains of the American Seamen, Soldiers, and Citizens, who perifhed on board the Jerfey Prifon Ship, during the Revolutionary War with Great Britain, and that we will cheerfully co-operate with the faid Society by all proper means in carrying the fame into effect.

Refolved, That
be and they hereby are appointed a Committee on the part of the Common Council for the pur-

pofe of conferring with the Committee of Tammany Society, and forming general arrangements
on the fubjects mentioned in the foregoing refolution.

ABRAHAM KING,[40]

ABRAHAM BLOODGOOD.[41]

New-York, March 28, 1808.

Ordered, That the preceding report be approved of, and that Alderman King, Alderman
Miller,[42] and Mr. Bloodgood, be the Committee accordingly.

Extract from the minutes,

JOHN PINTARD, Clerk.[43]

New-York, March 14, 1808

Sir,

I am defired by the prefiding officers and
members of Jerufalem Chapter of Royal Arch
Mafons, to acknowledge the receipt of the letter

you did them the honour to write in behalf of Tammany Society, and to exprefs their pleafurable concurrence in the meritorious and patriotic intention of Tammany Society to inter the relics of thofe Citizens who perifhed in the glorious caufe of liberty and independence on board the Jerfey Prifon Ship.

As moft of the members compofing Jerufalem Chapter are attached to the different lodges in the city, under the jurifdiction of the worfhipful the Grand Lodge, they will, with their refpective Lodges, cheerfully co-operate in the meafures to be adopted by their brothers.

I have the honour to be, with due confideration,

Your moft obedient fervant,

Joel Hart,[a]

Secretary of Jerufalem Chapter.

Robert Townfend, junr.

Secretary to the Committee of

Tammany Society.

Albany, April 4, 1808.

Dear Sir,

I have the pleafure of informing you, that the bill I brought into the Senate on your and Major Aycrigg's petition, with regard to the interment of the remains of the American Citizens who perifhed in the Jerfey Prifon Ship, &c., paffed the Senate this morning, and that the fum appro‑ priated for this humane object is four thoufand dollars. The oppofition was feeble, and the bill paffed almoft unanimoufly.

I am, dear Sir, with great refpect,

Your moft obedient fervant,

DE WITT CLINTON. [**]

Benjamin Romaine, Efq.

Note—The bill, as altered by the Affembly, and which paffed into a law, appropriates the fum of one thoufand dollars, to be raifed by the fale of public lands.

New-York, April 25, 1808.

Sir,

I have the honour to acknowledge the receipt of your letter, on the part of the Committee of Tammany Society, inclofing their Circular.

Agreeably to your requeft, I laid the fame before the company under my command, and have the pleafure to inform you, that they view the meafures adopted by the Committee as highly patriotic and humane, and reflecting lafting honour on the Society who originated them, as they will be the means of tranfmitting to the lateft pofterity an event highly interefting, and which will be engraven on the heart of every true American. They will, therefore, co-operate in fuch arangements as may be made for rendering military honours to thofe patriotic, but unfor-

tunate Americans, who were facrificed to Britifh
vengeance on board the Prifon Ships of the
enemy.

I am, Sir, your's with refpect,

CLARKSON CROLIUS,^(**)

Captain Friendfhip Volunteers.

Robert Townfend, junr.

Secretary of Committee of

Tammany Society.

New-York, May 2, 1808.

Sir,

The honour of your letter, dated February 24,
together with the Circular Letter of the Tammany Society of 11th February laft, have been
duly received and communicated to the company
under my command; they will cheerfully co-
operate with your Society in their laudable intention, and will attend the proceffion at fuch time
as fhall be appointed.

At the fame time, convinced that under the orders of the commanding officer of the corps, more military regularity might be expected, they fhould be happy to learn that he has alfo been invited to attend.

In behalf of the Company,

J. HEWETT, Capt.^(*)

Robert Townfend, junr.
Secretary of Wallabout Committee.

Note—The Committee will here ftate, that Brigadier General Morton, and Brigadier General Steddiford were invited, and that they gave the moft prompt and active affiftance at the funeral folemnities.

Firft Light Infantry Regiment.

New-York, May 5, 1808.

Sir,

I received, on the 20th ult. per poft, the com-

9

munication the Committee of Tammany Society
did me the honour to make, under date of February 24, and immediately laid it before my
Colonel, requeſting his permiſſion to comply
with the invitation. He has been pleaſed to
aſſent: myſelf and company will therefore join,
under correſpondent feelings, in the funeral
honours to be rendered the remains of the truly
brave American Citizens, Soldiers, and Seamen,
who, with rare fortitude, preferred to periſh
obſcurely, under all the horrors of tyranny, rather
than abandon the cauſe of Freedom and their
country.

I have the honour to be, very reſpectfully,

Your obedient ſervant,

CHARLES CHRISTIAN.

Robert Townſend, junr.
Secretary of the Committee of
Tammany Society.

United States Ship Conſtitution,[*]
Wallabout, May 18, 1808.

Sir,

I have the honour to acknowledge the receipt of your letter of yeſterday, and to aſſure you, that the ſentiments contained in it, relative to my motive for declining to take any part in the performance of the funeral ſolemnities, intended to take place on the 25th inſt. at the Wallabout, as a tribute of reſpect to the remains of our unfortunate fellow-countrymen who periſhed on board the Jerſey Priſon Ship, does me no more than juſtice.

The ground for my heſitation to take a part in theſe ceremonies being now ſatisfactorily removed, by your expreſſing that they are free from party motives; I am conſequently at liberty now, Sir, to expreſs to the honourable Committee of Tammany Society, through you, that their wiſhes ſhall be complied with, with infinite pleafure, fo far as refpects my co-operation, on that day, with their views.

I have the honour to be,

With great refpect, Sir,

Your obedient fervant,

John Rodgers.[*]

Robert Townfend, junr., Efq.

New-York, May 20, 1808.

Sir,

Yours of the 24th February laft, covering a Circular, relative to the Interment of the remains of our unfortunate countrymen who perifhed on board the Jerfey Prifon Ship, was received by me on the 20th April, ult.

Agreeable to the requeft therein contained, a meeting of my Company was had, when your letter was laid before them. I have to communicate to the Committee of Tammany Society, that I heartily concur in opinion with them, as to the propriety of the meafure, and that it is the refolve of the Company under my command to co-operate with them in their prefent undertaking.

I have delayed my anfwer until this time in order to afcertain the determination of General Morton, whofe coincidence with the requeft of the Committee has obviated the neceffity of my being informed of the arrangements, &c., to be made with regard to the military. I am, very refpectfully, Sir,

Your obedient fervant,

JOHN FLEMING.[60]

Robert Townfend, junr., Efq.

New-York, April, 1808.

Sir,

The underfigned, being a Committee appointed by Capt. Solomon D. Townfend, and the Company under his command, to take into confideration the letter addreffed by you to

Lieut. Pinkney, relative to the interment of the relics of American Seamen, Soldiers, and Citizens, who glorioufly facrificed their lives in defence of American liberty, on board the Jerfey Prifon Ship at the Wallabout, during the Revolutionary War, do moft cordially approve of the patriotic meafures adopted by the Committee of the Tammany Society, and will cheerfully co-operate with them in a caufe fo highly honourable to every friend of American independence.

Signed in behalf of the Company,

G. W. BROWN,[61]

GEORGE ENGLEHART,

RICHARD SMITH.

Robert Townfend, junr., Efq.
Secretary of Wallabout Committee.

Navy-Yard, New-York, April 5, 1808.
Sir,
I have the honour to acknowledge the receipt

of your letter of the 24th of laſt month, and highly approve of the humane and patriotic reſolution of the Tammany Society, of interring the relics of our countrymen who periſhed in the defence of our liberty, and which have long been toſſed and expoſed on the ſhores of the Wallabout; for which purpoſe I with great ſatisfaction add my mite, with that of the officer and detachment under my command.

I am, Sir, very reſpectfully,

Your obedient ſervant,

JOHN JOHNSON,

Lieut. Marines.

Robert Townſend, junr., Eſq.
Secretary of Wallabout Committee.

New-York, April 23, 1808.

Sir,

Yours of the 24th February, encloſing the Circular iſſued by the Tammany Society, or Columbian Order, has been duly received, and,

agreeably to requeſt, ſubmitted to the conſideration of the officers of the firſt Regiment of
Militia, under my command. I have the honour to inform the Committee, through you,
Sir, that the officers are highly ſenſible of the
propriety of perpetuating the remembrance of
thoſe ill-fated " American Brothers," whoſe
"known attachment" to their country's cauſe
procured them not only ſlavery, but an ignominious and untimely death, and whoſe bones
have too long been ſuffered to "bleach and
whiten in the northern blaſt."

But, Sir, as it is not in my power, as commandant of the Regiment, to adopt any official
meaſure, not particularly ſanctioned by law, and
by which I might poſſibly incur the cenſure (to
ſay the leaſt) of thoſe to whom, in a military
ſenſe, I am ſubordinate, I beg leave to inform
you, that no order has been taken on the communication above alluded to, farther than that
the officers agree to co-operate with the Society

in fuch way as their individual capacities and local arrangements may fuggeft, and which it may be in their power to do, conformably to any future order or plan of the Society.

For myfelf, Sir, I beg leave to offer to the Committee my acknowledgments for their polite expreffions of refpect; and while a figh of regret is prompted for the miferies of the long-departed victims of an unjuft war againft the liberties of my country, I beg you to believe I applaud every effort which may tend to render their names and memory immortal. You will pleafe to accept the enclofed as my mite towards the expence of the undertaking, and believe me to be, with refpect,

Your obedient, humble fervant,

DANIEL DODGE,[82]

Lieut. Col. Com'dt 1ft Regiment.

Robert Townfend, junr., Efq.
Secretary of Wallabout Committee.

10

New-York, May 29, 1808.

Brothers,

I feel proud at this particular feafon of having arrived among you ; your civilities, although of a diftant tribe, cannot be too highly appreciated, nor can the memory of the caufe which brought me to your wigwam ever be forgotten.

Brothers, I more than fympathize with you on the occafion; I loft a *Father*,—he was your *Brother*,—he was amongft the warriors who fought againft our common enemy :—And perhaps there remains nothing to be done to perpetuate their memory after what you have performed.

Inclofed is a fmall note, which I hope you will be pleafed to accept; it is the mite of an overflowing heart; and although forrowful the memory, yet may it ever be the means of ftrengthening the *link* and brightening the *hatchet* againft the enemies of the *liberties* of man.   I alfo, agreeably to your Circular of the 11th of February laft, communicate fuch circumftances refpecting my deceafed father, as I am at prefent in poffeffion of.

His name was Ezekiel Worrell. He was born at the burrow of Frankford, five miles north of the city of Philadelphia, in the ftate of Pennfylvania, on the 21ft of November, 1737; he took an active part in our Revolutionary War againft the enemies and oppreffors of his native country, and ferved as an officer in feveral reputable ftations amongst the militia thereof, at the battles of Prince-town, German-town, &c.

He was with Wafhington's army at White Marfh, in the neighbourhood of Philadelphia. Solicited to return to the bofom of his family, he replied, "*No*," (God blefs him!) "*I will remain here, and perifh, rather than difgrace myfelf under a Britifh flag.*" The Britifh left Philadelphia; he returned to his family, and there was induced by

a friend and family connection of his, a Capt.
Day, to go with him on board the privateer fhip
Revenge, from which he was taken, and put on
board the *fatal* Prifon Ship Jerfey. He there
ftill remained firm in his country's honour; for
he was again folicited by fome friends of his from
Philadelphia, who came, and were with the
Britifh, then in New-York; but he refufed—
and in their loathfome dungeon he *expired*.

Be pleafed to make fuch ufe of this narrative
as you may think moft proper, and oblige

Your brother and well-wifher,

JOSEPH WORRELL.[11]

To the Grand Sachem and
Tammany Society, New-York.

 R O M the unexpected zeal
manifested by the public, and
the individual exertions that
were made in promoting the
object for which the Commit-
tee were appointed, they were induced, at a much
earlier period than they had originally contemplated, to commence the building of the Vault.
On Wednefday, April 13, 1808, agreeably to
notice previoufly iffued by them, in purfuance of
a refolution of the Tammany Society, the corner-
ftone was laid.   The proceffion which took place
on the occafion was formed at the old ferry,
(Brooklyn)[*] at about half-paft 11 o'clock, A. M.,

and marched up Main-ſtreet,[65] through Sands',
Bridge, York, and Jackſon ſtreets to the ground,
in the following order, under the directions of
Major Aycrigg,[66] Grand Marſhal of the day :—

1. A company of United States Marines,
under the command of Lieut.-Commandant
Johnſon.

2. A body of Citizens.

3. Committees of different Societies.

4. The Grand Sachem of Tammany Society,
the Father of the Council, and the Orator of
the day.

5. The Wallabout Committee, preceded by
the corner-ſtone, drawn on a carriage.

6. A detachment of Captain Buckmaſter's
company of Artillery, under the command of
Lieutenant Townſend.

When the front of the proceſſion arrived at
the ground, it opened to the right and left, and
the remainder marched up in inverted order.

The detachment of Artillery filed off, and took poft on a hill adjacent to the place of inter-ment.[87] The colours being planted, and the company of Marines having taken their ftation, Benjamin Romaine,[88] Grand Sachem of the Tammany Society, accompanied by the mafter builders and the Tammany Committee, perform-ed the ceremony of laying the corner-ftone of the vault. The eye of every fpectator was anx-ioufly turned upon the fcene. The moft pro-found filence prevailed. It was a moment big with patriotic, and exalted and enthufiaftic feel-ings. It feemed that the recollections and fenfi-bilities of America were concentrated—and that the debt of gratitude to the memory of 11,000 of her brave but unfortunate defenders, which it belonged to the nation to difcharge, was about to be cancelled.

The following is the infcription upon the ftone:

" *In the name of the Spirits of the departed Free—Sacred*
to the Memory of that portion of American Seamen, Soldiers,
and Citizens, who perished on board the Prison Ships of the
British at the Wallabout during the Revolution.

" This is the corner-ftone of the vault erected
by the Tammany Society, or Columbian Order,
which contains their remains. The ground for
which was beftowed by John Jackfon—Naffau
Ifland,(") feafon of bloffoms. Year of the dif-
covery the 316th, of the inftitution the 19th, and
of American Independence the 32d. *April* 6,
1808.

"Jacob Vandervoort,
   John Jackfon,
   Burdett Stryker,
   Ifachar Cozzins,   } *Wallabout Com-*
   Robert Townfend, junr.   *mittee.*
   Benjamin Watfon,
   Samuel Cowdrey,

      David & Wm. Campbell, Builders."

Immediately after the ftone was laid the corps of Marines and the detachment of Artillery, difcharged by alternate firings, a national falute, in honour of the occafion. A folemn air was then performed by the band of martial mufic. The corps of Marines wheeled in front of the ftand erected for the orator. The detachment of Artillery furrounded the fame, and the citizens, to the number of nearly two thoufand, forming a circle around the fcite of the vault. JOSEPH D. FAY, Efq.[80] a member of the Tammany Society, having been appointed for that purpofe, then rofe and addreffed the affemblage in a fpeech highly animated and appropriate. The pictures which he drew of the fufferings of the heroes and martyrs of American liberty, were painted to the life. The feelings and fentiments of former times were revived at his defcriptions. Many of the furvivors of Britifh cruelty were prefent, and to the tears of fympathy which others fhed, added

11

thofe of bitter remembrance. The orator had many circumftances in his favour, and he could not fail to improve them. Before him "rolled the wave, which had once been darkened by the black hulks of Britifh Prifon Ships," on board of which many of the beft patriots of America had perifhed by ftarvation, by poifon, torture and every refinement of cruelty which the moft malignant ingenuity could inflict. He faw the fpot where their bones had been "bleached and mingled with fhells and fea weeds on the fhore," and the tomb which had been opened to receive them. The air was ferene—the fky unclouded—Nature appeared to liften and approve. The introduction which he made was beautifully concife and energetic.

"This day," faid the fpeaker, "we place the corner ftone of the tomb of the valiant. Too long has America ungratefully neglected to pay the tribute due to the braveft martyrs in the caufe of liberty."

He then adverted to the general fufferings of American prifoners, and inftituted a comparifon between their fituation and that of thofe of the enemy—and fhewed, that "while *fpare and be merciful* was the injunction of the brave heroes of America, the enemy feemed to fay, We know no mercy for rebels, and we fpare no *rebel* who has dared to oppofe us." He made honourable mention of thofe of the Britifh commanders who were diftinguifhed for their oppofition to the general fyftem of cruelty which prevailed, though he could not conceal the indignation which he felt, when he confidered, that "the fpirits of thoufands had flown to Heaven in confequence of barbarities exercifed in oppofition to the will of that God of battles whom Britons affected to adore." From general defcriptions, over which the minds of his hearers might pafs too haftily, or which, from the multiplicity and complication of the groups which compofed them, might pre-

sent no precise object on which to dwell, he de-
scended to more minute and circumstantial relations. He described the fate of the brave Colonel
Hayne⁽⁾ in a manner the most pathetic and
affecting.

"He fell into the hands of the British in 1781.
Lord Rawdon and *Colonel Balfour* resolved to execute him without a trial, and Colonel Hayne was
informed of the destiny which awaited him, two
days before it was to take effect. This cruel
determination having no law to sanction it, and
being made in defiance of every tender dictate of
the heart, awakened the sensibility of America.
The commissioned officers under General Green
addressed a well written petition, recommending
retaliation, hoping by that means to prevent the
cruelty. Many of the English officers themselves
made zealous efforts in his favour. Even beauty
engaged in his behalf; for, to the honour of
America let it be known, that her daughters have

diſplayed, in the cauſe of liberty and humanity, a more than Grecian Virtue. Alas, neither the ſtern petition of unbending valour, nor the melting prayer of ſoft eyed beauty, could touch the ſteeled heart of Rawdon, or turn him a moment from his cruel purpoſe. Hayne took affecting leave of his wife and relatives, and his laſt words to his ſon were, 'place me decently in the tomb, and *remember my enemies.*'"

Paſſing on to the particular occaſion of his addreſs, he thus eloquently deſcribed the fate of thoſe victims of Britiſh cruelty.

"But the ſufferings of thoſe unfortunate Americans whom the dreadful chances of war had deſtined for the Priſon Ships, were far greater than any which have been told. In that deadly ſeaſon of the year, when the dog-ſtar rages with relentleſs fury, when a pure air is ſpecially eſſential to health, and even the boſom of indolent eaſe, pants to catch it from the '*turret* and the *hill,*'

the Britifh locked their prifoners (after long
marches) in the dungeons of a fhip, infected with
contagion and reeking with the filth of crouded
captives *dead* and *dying*. In vain did the terrified
prifoner remonftrate and beg for pity. He was
hurled alive, without mercy, into this naufeous
grave—and no reafoning, no praying could obtain
from his ftern tyrants the fmalleft alleviation of
his fate. Yet there was one condition upon
which he might be fpared the torture of this flow
but certain death—and that was, enliftment in
the fervice of the enemy. To drive the American prifoners into this meafure was one motive
for fuch extraordinary cruelty. And to fee with
what remorfelefs ingenuity the lafh of torture was
wielded on the one hand, and the firmnefs with
which patriotifm endured it on the other, ftrikes
the mind with admiration and aftonifhment.

"In one inftance in South Carolina, after every
artifice which cunning could devife had been ufed

to perfuade the American prifoners to enlift, after
the Britifh officer called *Frafer* had in vain attempted to feduce them by hope and terrify them
with threats, he pronounced to them this ever to
be remembered denunciation:—"Go then," faid
he, "to your dungeons in the Prifon Ships, where
you fhall *perifh* and *rot*; but firft let me tell you,
that the rations which have been hitherto allowed
for your wives and children, fhall, from this
moment, ceafe for ever! and you fhall die affured
that *they* are ftarving in the public ftreets, and
that *you* are the *authors* of their fate." A fentence fo terribly awful, appalled the firm foul of
every liftening hero. A folemn filence followed
the declaration; they caft their wondering eyes
one upon the other, and valour for a moment
hung fufpended between love of family and love
of country; love of country at length rofe fuperior to every other confideration, and moved
by one impulfe, this glorious band of patriots

thundered in the aftonifhed ears of their perfecu-
tors, *The Prifon Ships and Death, or Wafhington
and our Country*. So magnanimous a refolve, one
would fuppofe, muft have extorted admiration
from the moft unfeeling enemy, and melted the
heart of even the untaught favage into tendernefs
and love. Not fo with thefe *moral* warriors in
the caufe of kings. Nero relented becaufe his
captive was brave. And Dyonifius wept and
pardoned the magnanimous fufferer in the caufe
of friendfhip. But the virtuous and unexampled
firmnefs of American heroes, ferved only to increafe the rage of their foes, and meagre famine
fhook hands with haggard peftilence, joining a
league to appal, conquer and deftroy the glorious
fpirit of liberty."

In defcribing the unfeeling conduct of "*one
Cunningham*"[*] he thus pourtrays, among others,
an inftance of his atrocity.

"This fame wretch ordered his minions to

ftrip the clothes from the back of the wife of an American foldier, and caufed her to receive many lafhes on the naked body, for no other crime than that fhe wept at the fufferings inflicted on her imprifoned hufband."

The orator here threw his whole foul into his voice and exclaimed :—

"Why fell not the red bolt of Heaven on the heads of thefe monfters in the fhape of men? Why did the vengeance of God fleep for a moment upon their bloody crimes? Dark and myfterious are the ways of Providence, and cannot be queftioned!" He then continued :— "As to the fufferings of thofe who expired in the Prifon Ships, it will be impoffible for the pen to defcribe, or the tongue to utter them. We may tell you that he who had breathed the pure breezes of the ocean, and had danced lightly in the flower-fcented air of the meadow and the hill, was on a fudden transferred to the pent-up

12

air of a Prifon Ship, pregnant with putrid fever, and deadly with naufeous contagion. There, in confinement and flavery, without one morfel of food to fatisfy hunger, without one drop of water to quench the burning fever of his tongue, he lingered out the tedious, weary day, and anxious, dreadful night, hopeful that death would kindly come and releafe him from mifery. He fainted in the fultry heat of fummer, and fhivered in the mercilefs blaft of winter. If drink was allowed him, it was deadly as the "green mantle of the ftanding pool;" and for nourifhment—they gave him poifon. Peftilence and famine could not fubdue him—but poifon! poifon was faithful! See the hero of America marching againft the invaders of his *land*—bold in the juftice of his caufe, appealing to the God of battles, and flufh-ed with the hopes of victory. By the myfterious power of Heaven, he is cloven down in the field, and hurried, with his wounds frefh bleeding, on board the black hulk which darkens yonder wave. As yet health blooms on his cheek, and the vigour of a robuſt conſtitution gives grace to his manly form. With an eye of proud diſdain he looks upon his tyrant keepers, and ſpurns with contempt the inſulting offer of eaſe, and liberty, on the terms of enliſtment under his enemy's banners. Confident in his ſtrength and his fortitude, he believes that the oppreſſor's arm can never ſubdue him. Alas! the hour rapidly approaches when his manly form ſhall wither on the ſhore—and dogs and eagles ſhall devour it. The ſun ſets in the weſtern wave, and darkneſs rolls about the head of the captive—" ſilent he liſtens to the founding main"—and ſighs as he thinks on the high-boſomed partner of his heart. He riſes in the fury of his madneſs, and hopes· for means to eſcape. Alas! there is no hope! The unfeeling ſentinel, faithful to his truſt, paces the deck with an ever watchful eye—the priſoner

groans out his life unpitied, unattended!—and
the watchman halloos to the paffing hour of the
night, that "all is well"!—Hear you not the
loud roar of revelry and untimely mirth; the
burft of noify joy which iffued from the cabin?
The keepers of the prifoners are feafting on deli-
cious viands—and thofe peals of laughter are
intended to reach the ear of the rebel. The wine
and the fong—the blood of the victim, and the
groan of the captive, are mingled at a feaft; and
famine, and peftilence attend as fervants. It is
no fable. Alas! it is too faithful a picture of
the manner in which *eleven thoufand heroes* have
perifhed!! Think, fellow-citizens, what would
be your fenfations were you thus called upon to
fuffer in your country's caufe? and you, ye
white-armed daughters of America, bright in
your beauty, whofe "eyes like ftars look forward
through a rufhing fhower," how could you bear
to reflect on the fpirit of a hufband and lover
thus wounded and broken down?

" More than five and twenty years have rolled
away since those heroes fell "like groves in the
desert, when an angry ghost rushes through the
night and takes their green heads in his hand."

" They preferred a terrible death to a derelic-
tion of principle, and their names are not known
to Americans! They suffered, when no eye could
admire, and no voice praise; yet their relics have
not had the rites of sepulture! They might have
added eleven thousand *terrible* soldiers (for terrible they must have been) to the already too
powerful enemy of America. They chose to die
rather than injure the republic. And the republic hath never yet paid them the tribute of
gratitude!

" On this day we lay the corner stone of their
tomb. Their ashes hitherto have been blown
about like "summer's dust in the whirlwind."
But the marble column shall rise on this spot,
and tell to future ages the story, that they had

to choofe death or flavery, and that they nobly
elected the former. Perhaps their fpirits are this
moment on "the wings of the wind," hovering
over our heads, and fmiling on the pious tribute
we now humbly pay to their memories. In this
fepulchre fhall their white bones be gathered. It
fhall overlook the fcene of their probation, and
be at once a monument of American gratitude,
and of Englifh barbarity. The curious mariner
fhall point at it in filent admiration as he paffes
at a diftance, and pofterity fhall call it ' THE
TOMB OF THE PATRIOTS.' "

To ftate the effects which this addrefs had on
the audience is almoft impoffible—fuffice it to
fay, that it produced alternately the tear of re-
fined fenfibility, the filence of indefcribable and
unutterable indignation, and repeated burfts of
applaufe.

The orator having concluded, the proceffion

returned in inverfe order to the place of rendez-
vous, formed a circle round the Liberty Pole,
near the market,[*] gave three cheers, and retired.

H E Tomb of the Martyrs be-
ing completed, the Tammany
Society intended that the bones
of thofe patriots who expired in
the Prifon Ships fhould be con-
figned to the fepulchre on Wednefday, the 25th
May, 1808;[*] but a heavy ftorm of rain prevented it. On Thurfday, the 26th, the early
morn promifed a fair day, and the firft ray of
twilight was announced by a morning gun from
the Park—the Battery—Fort Columbus—the
Flotilla—and the Wallabout. The thunder of
the cannon re-echoed from fhore to fhore, and
died away in murmurs along the waters of the

Eaſt river and the Hudſon. It was the dawn of a day, glorious to America. The patriot was awake—his boſom felt the ſolemnity inſpired by the echo of cannon ; he turned back his mind to the time when ſimilar ſounds conveyed terror to the now peaceful city, and were accompanied with death and conflagration. As ſoon as the morning guns had ceaſed to fire, the reveille was ſounded from all the different military poſts in the city and its neighbourhood. At ſunriſe, at all the public places in the city—at all military poſts— and on all veſſels (excepting the Britiſh) were diſplayed the American flag, and the flags of different nations, at half maſt. Minute guns were fired from different quarters. The bells of the city and of the ſhipping, pealed the ſolemn funeral toll, ſounding to the patriotic American a moſt pathetic language. Every where were ſeen men and women walking to and fro—the ſtreets of the city ſwarmed with people—the military

and public bodies began to affemble—officers and
foldiers were paffing and repaffing to their different pofts—and beauty crowded the windows of
thofe houfes by which the proceffion was to pafs,
watching in folemn filence the firft movement of
the line. A grand Funeral Proceffion, marching
to the Tomb of Martyrs who died in the caufe
of freedom—a nation rifing up, "fhaking its
invincible locks," wiping off the afperfion of ingratitude, and bending with a humble piety before the relics of heroes—this is a mighty theme!

At ten o'clock, under the command of General Morton[a] and General Steddiford,[b] all the
military, and the citizens, focieties, &c. under
the direction of Garret Sickles,[c] Grand Marfhal of the day, formed the proceffion in Broadway. The Grand Marfhal was aided by twelve
fubaltern Marfhals. The proceffion then moved
forward in the following order.

I.

A Trumpeter, mounted on a Black Horfe, dreffed in character, (black relieved with red,) wearing a helmet ornamented with flowing black and red feathers; in his right hand a trumpet, to which was fufpended a black filk flag, edged with red and black crape, on which appeared the following memorable *Motto*, in letters of gold.

MORTALS AVAUNT!

11,500

SPIRITS OF THE MARTYRED BRAVE,

APPROACH THE TOMB OF HONOUR, OF GLORY, OF

VIRTUOUS PATRIOTISM!

II.

Colonel Vanzandt, Chief Herald, in full military drefs, mounted on an elegant White Horfe, richly caparifoned, bearing the ftaff and cap of liberty, to which was fufpended an elegant blue filk fhield, edged with red and black crape;

the field covered with thirteen ftars in gold, emblematic of the original American conftellation.

III.

Major Aycrigg as a Citizen, and Captain Coffin (**) as a naval character, acted as aids or fupporters to the Chief Herald, in plain black
dreffes, wearing feathers and red fafhes, the
horfes &c. uniform, each carrying a filken flag of
the American ftripes, with crape, &c.

IV.

An Efcort of Horfe, (preceded by a Trumpet,)
under the command of Major Warner.

V.

A Detachment of Field Artillery, under the
command of Captain Buckmafter.

VI.

Brigadier General Morton, accompanied by

his Aids, commanding the Firſt Grand Diviſion
of the Military, compoſed of Artilleriſts, with
ſmall arms, colours, band of muſic, drums and
fifes, military mourning, &c. agreeable to the
rules of war. This valuable body of citizen
ſoldiers appeared to uncommon advantage on
this ſolemn occaſion; they marched with re-
verſed arms, being the cuſtom on all funeral oc-
caſions.

VII.

Brigadier General Steddiford accompanied by
his Aids, &c. commanding the Second Grand
Diviſion, compoſed of various bodies of Infantry,
each corps under the particular charge of their
own commandant; their noble, martial, and
truly ſoldierly conduct on ſo ſolemn an occaſion,
has rivetted to them the affections and eſteem
of their fellow citizens, eſpecially *Capt. Commandant McClures* corps, the *Republican Greens*, which

appeared more brilliant and numerous than on any former occafion : their unrivaled *volunteer band of mufic* deferves unbounded praife ; they were the firft to perform the *Grand Wallabout Dead March*, which has done much honour to the compofer, *Captain James Hewitt.* A Detachment of Artillery and a Squadron of Horfe brought up the rear of this Divifion.

VIII.

A Band of Mufic, occafionally performing the Grand Wallabout Dead March, the inftruments, &c. all relieved with red and black crape.

IX.

This place was intended for the Cincinnati.[*] Time having reduced this veteran band to a very fmall number, all who attended were diftributed among the military and other honourable bodies, in which they held ftations.

X.

The Grand Marſhal, Garret Sickels, appropriately drefſed, with feather, faſh, &c. bearing a
trunchion in his hand, accompanied by four Aids,
each mounted on horſeback, appropriately drefſed,
wearing blue faſhes, feathers, &c. and carrying a
white ſilk banner.

XI.

The Clergy, in their cuſtomary order. The
Rev. Mr. Townly[n] and the Rev. Mr. Williſ-
ton,[n] were the only two of that refpeċtable body
who appeared with the Proceffion in the city : at
Brooklyn they were joined by the Rev. Mr.
Striker and the Rev. Mr. Van Neſt of New-
Jerſey.

XII.

The Wallabout Committee, ſeven in number,
each wearing in his hat the buck tail,[n] as a dif-

tinguifhing mark of their being members of
Tammany Society or Columbian Order, dreffed
in black, with a broad red badge, relieved with
crape, fufpended from the neck, and a badge of
mourning round the left arm.

XIII.

Tammany Society or Columbian Order, and
the Thirteen Coffins, filled with the Bones of
immolated American Patriots: the following is
the order in which the Society marched.

1*ft*, The Cap of Liberty, fhrouded in crape,
carried by the Wifkinkie.[73]

2*nd*, The Great Standard of the Society, fupported by the Sagamore and his two Mafters of
Ceremonies. This Standard is of an oval form;
it fhews the arms of the United States, emblazoned on both fides; a margin of eight inches
round it exhibits to view the thirteen animals by
which each tribe is reprefented; the outer edge

is decorated with a profufion of elegant feathers, in the Mexican ftyle; it is fufpended to a ftaff, on the top of which is a large plume of feathers— the whole was overhung with crape. The Mafters of Ceremonies, one on each fide the Sagamore, held by a taffel the end of a filken label, on which is written in golden letters,

'TAMMANY SOCIETY OR COLUMBIAN ORDER.'

3rd, The Grand Sachem, wearing the badge of his office. This badge is a filver chain, compofed of thirteen links, within each link is a ftar; a gold medal is fufpended from it, on which appears the flame of liberty dedicated to freedom; its motto—'Preferve by Concord.' The Grand Sachem was fupported by the Treafurer on his right, carrying wampum, and the Secretary on his left, carrying the journal of the Society.

4th, The Orator, in a plain black drefs.

5th, Father of the Council, fmoaking the

14

calumet; on his right, the Scribe, carrying the conftitution, and on his left, the Counfellor, carrying the book of laws.

6*th*, The Sachem of the New-York tribe.

7*th*, The Standard bearer, carrying a banner, fhewing the arms of the State on one fide, and a ftar on the other, fufpended to a ftaff, furmounted with the cap of liberty, all covered with black.

8*th*, The Tribe Hunter.

9*th*, The body of the Tribe in two lines, leaving a fpace of fourteen feet between them; within this area the firft coffin was borne on men's fhoulders, over which appeared the American Flag; this invaluable relic is the identical flag which firft waved in triumph on the Battery, in place of the one which the Britifh left flying on the ever memorable 25th of November, 1783: the day the Immortal WASHINGTON entered the city at the head of his war-worn and almoft exhaufted, but virtuous army, and the Britifh turned their faces towards the eaft, leaving us at peace, free and independent.

10*th*, One hundred and four Revolutionary Characters, eight to each coffin, affifted as Pall Bearers; of thefe the honourable Samuel Of-good[74] and the honourable Henry Rutgers[75] were ftationed in front, on the right and left of the firft coffin; each of the Pall Bearers wore a large white fcarf, relieved with crape, &c. The Alank, or Clerk, brought up the rear of the Firft Tribe.

The New-Hampfhire, Maffachufetts, Rhode-Ifland, Connecticut, New-Jerfey, Pennfylvania, Delaware, Maryland, Virginia, North Carolina, South Carolina, and Georgia Tribes followed, each attending a coffin and marching in the fame order.

O Americans! here make a folemn paufe! thefe thirteen fmall receptacles now contain the manes of our country's virtuous martyred fons. Ye fires, ye matrons, ye youth of America—remember the fufferings they endured—indent them on the rocks—cut them on the trees—write them in indelible inks—and imprefs them on the minds of your offspring, that they may be remembered while our country bears the name of free.

XIV.

Mufic performing the dead march of the martyrs.

XV.

The Grand National Pedeftal. This fublime fpectacle confifted of an oblong fquare ftage, erected on a large truck carriage, the margin of which reprefented an iron railing; below this dropped a deep feftoon which covered the wheels; a pedeftal reprefenting black marble, eight feet long, fix feet high, and four wide, ſtood on the ſtage. On the four pannels or tablets, were the following inſcriptions:

(FRONT)

AMERICANS! REMEMBER THE BRITISH.

(RIGHT SIDE)

YOUTH OF MY COUNTRY! MARTYRDOM PREFER TO SLAVERY.

(LEFT SIDE)

SIRES OF COLUMBIA! TRANSMIT TO POSTERI-TY THE CRUELTIES PRACTISED ON BOARD THE BRITISH PRISON SHIPS.

(REAR)

TYRANTS DREAD THE GATHERING STORM,—WHILE FREEMEN, FREEMEN'S OBSEQUIES PERFORM.

On the top of the Pedeſtal was diſplayed a ſuperb blue ſilk flag, eighteen feet by twelve, on which were emblazoned, in the moſt ſuperior ſtyle, the arms of the United States ; on the top of the ſtaff, eighteen feet high, was a globe, on which ſat the American Bald Eagle, enveloped in a cloud of black crape—the noble Eagle ſeemed to mourn !

The GENIUS OF AMERICA was repreſented by Joſiah Falconer,[78] a member of Tammany Society, and the ſon of a Revolutionary patriot. This gentleman is a fine figure, and appeared to the greateſt advantage ; his dreſs was a looſe under dreſs of light blue ſilk, which reached to his knees, over which was a long flowing white robe, relieved by a crimſon ſcarf and crape ; he wore ſandals on his feet, and on his head a magnificent cap, adorned with the moſt elegant feathers which could be obtained, all in the Mexican ſtyle. On the ſtage, and round the pedeſtal, ſtood nine young gentlemen, each holding by a taſſel the end of a cord, which ſerved as a ſupport and ftay to the flag. Thefe young men reprefented—Patriotifm, Honour, Virtue, Patience, Fortitude, Merit, Courage, Perfeverance and Science; and were called, the Attributes of the Genius of America; they were all drefled in character, with a plume of feathers in their hats, a white filk fcarf, relieved with black crape; under the arm of each was fufpended a fcarlet badge, edged with elegant dark blue filk fringe, in the fhape of a crefcent, on which was written the name of the characters refpectively, in gold; each attribute alfo held in his hand a blue filk banner, emblematic of the inftitution to which he belonged. This beautiful ftructure was drawn by four horfes, under the charge of two Poftillions, drefled in ribbons and crape.—Genius of our country! the cloud which thirty years hung o'er thy brow, this day by mortals is removed!

XVI.

Neptune's hardy Sons—the American Tars, next followed, upwards of three hundred in number, in divifions of fifty, headed by an officer, two abreaft, the American flag, half maft, appeared at the head of each divifion ; they were dreffed in blue jackets, white trowfers, and round hats, wearing a crape band round the hat and left arm. Thefe brave Republicans of the ocean, to the contemplative mind, was a moft affecting fight—it was truly interefting indeed—that fight alone drew the fympathizing tear from every eye :—Thefe worthy, thefe patriotic tars, were infpired with one foul! they were fteady and true, as the needle to the pole ; the moft exact order, and the greateft harmony were obferved in their ranks.

XVII.

The Municipal Officers and Citizens of the

town of Brooklyn formed this divifion.⁽ᵐ⁾ The
Artillery, under Captain Boerum,⁽ⁿ⁾ took their
ftation, agreeably to the rules of war.

XVIII.

The honourable the Corporation of the city
of New-York next appeared in this grand, this
folemn fcene!—The honourable De Witt Clinton,
Mayor of the city, accompanied by the Recorder
and moft of the Aldermen and Affiftants, and
the officers attached to their body, preceded by a
numerous body of Conftables and Marfhals, carrying their ftaves of office.

XIX.

His excellency Daniel D. Tomkins,⁽ᵒ⁾ Governor of the State, his Aids and Suite, with the
honourable John Broome, Lieutenant Governor
—members of Congrefs, members of the Legiflature, Diplomatic and other characters of diftinc-

tion, including naval and military officers from various parts of the United States, and from foreign countries. It was a truly dignified and interefting fight, to fee the dignitaries of our country joined in the melancholy train, like freedom's fons, like wifdom's aids, following to the tomb the bleached bones which thirty years lay expofed on the dreary fhores of the Wallabout.

XX.

The Mechanic Society of the city of New-York, headed by their Prefident and other officers, two and two, difplaying the ftandard and other infignia of the inftitution, all appropriately dreffed in mourning, with crape on the left arm, &c.

XXI.

The Shipwrights, in their cuftomary order, preceded by their Prefident, attended by the fub-

officers, exhibiting a beautiful Standard, difplaying the Arms of their inftitution—banners, &c.
all appropriately dreffed in crape. Among this
invaluable body of citizens were feen fome living
witneffes of the *tender mercies* of the Britifh.

XXII.

Hibernia's Sons—noble, generous, brave—
The patriotic and charitable inftitution, the
Hibernian Provident Society,(°) with unaffected
and deep felt grief, here paffed along. The
Prefident and other officers in their proper ftations : the whole body wore the badge of their
Society, with crape on the left arm, &c. Their
elegant Standard, which fhews the arms of the
inftitution, and their country, with appropriate
banners, &c. being properly enfhrouded in
mourning. Here were beheld hundreds of
Erin's perfecuted fons—here were feen fons
whofe fathers' bones were as yet untomb'd! and

brothers to the yet unburied martyred brave!—
here were feen a band of patriots, many of whom
might fay, *There perifhed my Father by cruel
famine! There my wounded Friend by the bayonet's
plunge! There my fick, my dying Brother, devoured
in the flames of the STROMBOLO, in attempting in
vain to feek a watery grave.*

XXIII.

The Society of Coopers in their ufually orderly
and appropriate ftyle, their Prefident leading
them two by two, wearing the oak leaf in their
hats, their ftandard and banners difplayed, and
appropriately relieved with crape. This ufeful
band of citizens on all public occafions have ever
fhown an uncommon zeal; on this occafion they
reciprocated with their fellow citizens the fentiment of pious gratitude to the venerable dead.

XXIV.

In regular fucceffion followed the Society of

Mafons, two by two, with crape on the left arm, each wearing the medal, or badge of the inftitution; they were numerous and refpectable, headed by their Prefident. The arms of their Society were difplayed on an elegant filk flag, judicioufly ornamented with black.

XXV.

The ancient order of Taylors next advanced, headed by their Prefident, two by two, difplaying their ftandard, banners, &c. all wearing crape.

XXVI.

The Hatter's Society followed, two and two, wearing the emblem of their inftitution, fufpended from the button hole, on the left breaft, and crape on the left arm; they were led by their Prefident, accompanied by their officers. The ftandard and banners of this Society were all in appropriate mourning.

XXVII.

The laft of the Societies was the Concord.[81] This body, like all the preceding ones, appeared with ftandard, banners, infignia, &c. of the order, all dreffed in crape, the members walking in couples, each carrying a green branch in his hand, and wearing a band of crape on the left arm.

XXVIII.

Mufic—Grand and Solemn.

XXIX.

The Citizens, of all claffes, here in deep and folemn filence walk'd, four abreaft. This immenfe body moved with the utmoft regularity and order, each wearing crape on the arm, and carrying a cyprefs branch in the hand; they were conducted by two of the Grand Marfhal's Aids, mounted on horfeback, diftinguifhed by blue fafhes and flowing red and black feathers.

In this affemblage, compofed of the inhabitants of a large, opulent and enlightened city, all diftinctions of politics, of religion, of wealth, or family, were buried in the general fentiment of fympathizing forrow; all, like brothers of the fame family, joined hand in hand in paying the laft fad tribute at the confecrated tomb.

XXX.

The Military Officers off duty. This very refpectable body of citizens appeared in full military drefs. They walked two and two, each wearing crape on the left arm. A few of the remaining war worn veterans of the Revolution here were feen. The Great Spirit has preferved them from the tyrants grafp for deeds of future glory. In melancholy filence they followed the manes of their countrymen to the tomb of the patriots.

XXXI.

A Detachment of Field Artillery.

XXXII.

This fplendid proceffion was clofed by a troop of Horfe.

GREEABLE to arrangement, the proceffion marched from the Park down Broad-way, to Trinity church, thence, down Wall-ftreet to Pearl-ftreet, up Pearl-ftreet through Cherry-ftreet, to the New Market,[7] when the Military halted and opened to the right and left. The Societies and Citizens then marched thro' to their refpective places of embarkation.

The profpect here prefented was folemn and interefting. A body of troops, compofed of Cavalry, Infantry and Artillery, form a moving phalanx, taking their filent ftation, while the relics

16

of departed worth, attended by a numerous concourfe of citizens, pafs by.—The gallant Horfe-
man's lofty helmet drooping, and his head re-
clining on the firm hilt of his trufty fword—the
youthful Infantry, refting on their arms, now
mournfully reverfed—and the Conductors of Columbia's Thunder, colonnading the line—while
the awful ftillnefs which reigned was alone interrupted by the performance of the Wallabout
March, founding an infpiring requium to the
brave heroes of liberty. This was a fcene which
awakened the gratitude of the Revolution, and
excited veneration in every bofom for the memory of 'the Martyrs.' The young gazed with
wonder, and old age wept at the recollections it
infpired.

Boats for the embarkation were provided, at
different places on the Eaft river. Thirteen
large open boats tranfported the thirteen tribes of
Tammany Society, each containing one Tribe,
one Coffin, and the Pall Bearers.

The Grand Sachem, Father of the Council, and other officers not attached to tribes, accompanied by the Chief Herald, his Aids, and the Trumpeter led the van, the boats following in order.

The car was embarked on board a veffel conftructed for the purpofe, and tranfported under the management of feveral mafters of veffels, who volunteered their fervices: the Genius and fupporters retaining their ftations. This beautiful ftructure in its paffage attracted the notice of every eye. From the current it received a direction down the river, which made its courfe circuitous, defcribing a line of perfect beauty. The elegant ftandard floating in the wind, on which were feen the badges of each Society—the white robes loofely flowing around the tall and graceful figure of the Genius—and the cloud coloured pedeftal which fupported them, prefented to the imagination of every beholder an object of the moft pleafing admiration.

The honourable the Corporation, his excellency the Governor, the Lieut. Governor, and other officers of diſtinction, paſſed over in a very large open boat, elegantly accommodated for the occaſion, and dreſſed with colours at half maſt, awnings, &c.

All the other bodies, civil, military and naval, and the citizens at large, croſſed in boats prepared for the purpoſe.[*] The Republican Greens appeared to great advantage: they had their fine band on board the ſloop which conveyed them, continually playing an appropriate piece. The men arranged themſelves in ſingle file round the deck. The other military corps which paſſed over, are entitled to equal commendation, though they had not the advantage of muſic.

Fleets of ſmall craft were ſeen induſtriouſly plying to and from the city, extending from the ſouthern point of the city to Corlaer's Hook.[*]

Pleafure boats with their colours waving half
maft high, and ftreaming far out in the wind,
were failing fwiftly up and down the ftream.
Minute guns were fired from all quarters. At
a diftance were feen volumes of fmoke wheeling
up the fky, fucceeded in fhort intervals by the
roaring of the cannon. The arms of the
military gliftened in the fun from the heights of
Corlaer's Hook; and on the hills of Brooklyn
crowds of ladies eyed with ferious contemplation
the vaft grandeur of the fcene. The waters of
the Eaft river foamed beneath the oars of a
thoufand boats; the fails of a hundred veffels
fwelled to the breeze, and a mild fun feemed to
fmile benignantly on this interefting fcene. More
than thirty thoufand bofoms this day paid the
tribute of feeling to the memory of the Martyrs,
from that hill beneath whofe brow eleven thoufand had expired!

At Brooklyn Ferry the proceffion formed

again ; and here they were joined by very many citizens of Brooklyn. Several ladies added the grace of beauty to the line, and marched to the 'tomb of the valiant.'[*] It is impoſſible to deſcribe the intereſting effect of the proceſſion marching over the green hills of Brooklyn. The colors of the military waved in the wind, changing and turning to the ſound of ſlow and moſt impreſſive muſic. High floated the flag of America, as if triumphant that the ſtain of ingratitude was this day to be wiped away. The proceſſion ſtreamed along the valley and over the hill, and arrived at the tomb of the Martyrs, amidſt a vaſt and mighty aſſembly. A ſtage had been erected for the Orator, trimmed with black crape. The coffins were placed in front, and the pall bearers took their ſeats beneath the eye of the orator. The genius of America, 'high upon the car,' ſtood on his right. The Tammany Society arranged itſelf before him, and citizen be-

hind citizen covered the plain and the hill as far
as the profpect extended. A detachment of the
military marched to the fouth eaft bank of the
Eaft river with the cannon, from whence they
fired minute guns for fome time; and were an-
fwered by the thunder of Artillery from Corlaer's
Hook, Fort Columbus, and other military pofts.

The military ftanding on the brow of the diftant hill, dreffed as they were in complete uniform, appeared to uncommon advantage. Their
guns gleamed in the fun—the fmoke of their
cannon was feen rolling in mighty volumes towards Naffau, and directly was heard its fullen
thunder echoing along the fky, and dying away
in diftance. As foon as the firing ceafed, a
folemn filence pervaded the multitude, and ex-
pectation fat on every countenance. The coffins
remained uncovered—the tomb was opened to
receive them—the remains of American Martyrs
were about to be honoured with the rites of

fepulture. Thirty years had rolled away fince
they were fpurned into the fand like dogs by unfeeling tyrants; and this day, for the firft time,
a tear was dropped upon their relics. It was an
awful filence, like that of the ocean when it fleeps,
and the fun refts on the waters. The Rev.
RALPH WILLISTON, ftanding on the right of the
orator, then addreffed ' the God of battles' in a
moft folemn, eloquent and pious fupplication.
His heart fwelled with gratitude towards that
providence whofe hand guided America through
the dark ftorms of Revolutionary war, and
led her triumphantly to a lofty ftation among
the nations of the earth. Fired by his rapturous
duty, his imagination foared back to the time
when thofe martyrs lived, ' *the foe's dread terror,
and their country's hope.*' He fpoke of their fig-
nal fuffering, and prayed, that he who held the
balance of nations in his hand would teach the
fons of America to cherifh, as they would life,

that glorious boon of freedom which the martyrs and heroes of the Revolution had purchafed
' *with the facrifice of much blood.*'

*The following is a copy of Mr. Willifton's Addrefs,
as far as it could be recollected.*

"DREAD SOVEREIGN, fupreme, all-bountiful,
unchangeable and eternal. Thou art the Creator
of all things, and the Father of our fpirits: with
thee are the deftinies of all nations, and of all individuals; and thou art the rightful and fole
Governor of the univerfe. Under thy govern-
ance a nation fhall rife, profper, and obtain great
renown: but through her own infidelities and ingratitude, fhall decline and become inglorious.
It is through thy aufpices that we have become a
great nation. Much was the facrifice of time,
property, fufferings and ftrength, which fubferved
thy will in the accomplifhment of our national
independence and aggrandizement. Nor would

17

we remain unmindful of the fervices and fufferings of the patriots of our Revolution. Behold
from the heights of thy excellence this very numerous concourfe, called together to perform
fepulchral rites to the remains of thofe who
counted not their fervices, fufferings and deaths
too great a facrifice made in the attainment of
their country's emancipation. We thank thee
that we can recognize the glorious fame of holy
Martyrs, who fell in the caufe of the chriftian
religion, and that of thofe Revolutionary victims
who fell in the caufe of their country.

"We come, therefore, to dignify and render
efficient the fentiment of gratitude; the fentiment, religioufly venerated in paft ages; the
fentiment, which renders honour to whom honour is due; the fentiment, which will have in
everlafting remembrance the virtues, fervices and
fufferings of the benefactors of mankind. And
may we be accompanied with every fentiment

and difpofition fuited to the folemnities of the occafion. May nothing tranfpire incompatible with thefe folemnities. " Thou, Lord, knoweft the thoughts of our hearts ; fhut not thy merciful ear to our fupplications : but fpare us, Lord moft holy, and fuffer us not, at our laft hour, for any pains of death to fall from thee."

" We commend to thy fatherly goodnefs thefe United States. Suffer no evil machination, or weapon defigned againft them to profper. Preferve unto them all their rights and inftitutions. May they never be found devoid of patriotifm in the hour of danger ; and fhould their liberties at fome time become endangered, then may that invincible fpirit which directed the meafures, and fupported the patriots of the Revolution, infpire their fons with the true love of country ; with an invincible magnanimity, and with an unfhaken refolution, *to protect their liberties and the tombs of their patriots*, from the hoftile aggreffor, or to *perish themselves in the contest*. Yet, O All-bountiful! if it be poſſible, may theſe United States live in amity with all nations. To thy holy keeping we commit them, together with all the powers that be, beſeeching thee to teach all nations, that by thee kings rule and princes decree juſtice. And ſpeed the time when celeſtial peace, with balmy wings, ſhall ſhade and bedew the world.

"To the King Immortal, Inviſible, the All-wiſe God, be glory everlaſting. *Amen.*"

After this impreſſive prayer was finiſhed, Doctor BENJAMIN DE WITT[86] delivered the Funeral Oration, which he had prepared at the requeſt of the Tammany Society, in a ſtyle and manner dignified, pathetic and eloquent. He ſpoke of thoſe tyrants whoſe cruel treatment conſigned to death eleven thouſand patriots, and indignation ſhook the multitude. He deſcribed

the heroic fortitude with which the martyrs endured indeſcribable miſery ; and while the audience liſtened to catch the relation, tears of ſym-
pathy bedimmed their eyes. It was a ſolemn
and ſublime hour.

THE FOLLOWING IS THE

ORATION.

REAT GOD! are thefe the bones of my incarcerated countrymen? are thefe the remains of more than ten thoufand brave men who died in the caufe of liberty? have thefe relics of death continued for the fpace of thirty years uncovered with their native earth? and is there no reft for this facred duft, even in the habitations of the dead? is there no friendly hand to collect it—no friendly tomb to receive it?

O my country! while I mourn over this fcene

of human defolation, my foul fickens at thine ingratitude. Haft thou forgotten the fufferings of thy patriotic fons, who perifhed for thee in the dark days of thine affliction? haft thou forgotten the dead becaufe they can no longer ferve the living? No—thou couldft not forget—the Almighty, in his righteous difpleafure, forbade it—thefe dry bones have continually founded in thine ear the melancholy death of the Seaman and the Soldier who clung to thy banners in the hour of diftrefs: their ghaftly fkeletons have appeared before thee, a horrible fpectacle of the barbarity of thine enemy; and a voice from the grave hath admonifhed thee to perform the laft kind office of humanity to their remains, and of juftice to their memory.

This day then, fellow citizens, we are affembled to wipe away with our tears a ftain from our country's glory, and to do honour to the departed patriots of the Revolution. Too long, alas! have

the rites of fepulture been denied to thefe remnants of the bodies of the valiant, who died in
the conteft for freedom. But the time is come
when they fhall reft in the tomb of their fathers;
here fhall they be placed in the filent vault; and
here fhall the tear of fenfibility flow for their
fufferings.

But when thefe auguft funeral folemnities are
ended, fhall they but be covered with a green fod,
and remembered no more forever? fhall not their
names and their virtues be told to pofterity? Say
my countrymen, fhall the great man who furvives
the conteft and dies in the days of tranquillity and
peace, have his name enrolled on the page of
hiftory, and his virtues infcribed in the temple
of religion? and is there no place under the vault
of heaven to record the fufferings of the meritorious fons of liberty, who expired under the moft
dreadful calamities of war?—Shall the rich man,
who dies in luxury and fplendor, amidft the com-

forts of the world and the friends of his bofom,
have his name engraven on a coftly tomb? and
fhall no monumental marble tell the untimely
death of the poor patriotic tenants of a prifon;
who, rather than feaft on the fpoils of their
country, funk under the vengeance of a vindic-
tive foe? Nay, fhall even the tyrants, the unrelenting tyrants, who have ftrewed thefe bones
in the Wallabout; who have committed cruelty
on the living and facrilege on the dead; fhall
they fleep in magnificent monuments in their
native land? and fhall no ftone be erected here
to perpetuate the memory of thofe freemen who
fuffered martyrdom for their country?—Yes, they
fhall be remembered with affection—their names
fhall be immortal—the fpirit of feventy-fix hath
reanimated the fouls of our Revolutionary veterans, and kindled a flame of patriotifm in the
bofoms of the rifing generation. They fhall
unite their exertions to erect in this memorable

18

place, this field of blood, a monument of glory to the dead. Here fhall the brave fufferers in the Britifh Prifon Ships receive the juft tribute of everlafting fame to their memory.

How many American Seamen, Soldiers and Citizens died in thofe floating dungeons of the enemy, during the Revolutionary war, no man can tell. Thefe piles on piles of their mouldering bones can give us no adequate conception of their number.* From the dark caverns of the JERSEY fhip alone, it is computed that more than eleven thoufand dead bodies were depofited near this awful fpot.† How many were deftroyed by

* Near twenty hogfheads full of thefe bones had been collected by the indefatigable induftry of John Jackfon, efq. the Committee of Tammany Society, and other citizens, to be interred in the vault.

† The American Sailors, when captured by the Britifh, fuffered more than even the Soldiers which fell into their hands. The former were confined on board Prifon Ships; they were there crowded together in fuch numbers, and their accommodations were fo wretched, that difeafes broke out and fwept them off in fuch a manner, that it was fufficient to excite compaffion in

difeafes in the crowded prifons of the JOHN.
How many were poifoned in the peftilential at-
mofphere of the SCORPION.[87]   How many were
fuffocated in the fcuttled holds of the STROMBO-
LO[88]—How many were famifhed in the deadly
HUNTER*[89]—How many were transfixed by the
bayonets of the bloody guards—How many were
devoured in the flames of the burning *Tranfport*†

breafts of the leaft fenfibility.   It has been afferted, on as good evidence as
the cafe will admit, that in the laft fix years of the war, upwards of eleven
thoufand perfons died on board the Jerfey, one of the Prifon Ships which
was ftationed in the Eaft river, near New-York.   On many of thefe, the
rites of fepulture were never, or but very imperfectly conferred.   For fome
time after the war ended, their bones lay whitening in the fun on the fhores
of Long-Ifland."

Ramfay's Hiftory of the Revolution, vol. 2, p. 284.

* See Freneau's Poem on the Prifon Ships.

† A Britifh veffel in the Wallabout, faid to contain about three hundred
American prifoners, which took fire and was confumed.   As fhe burnt the
men were feen letting each other down from the port holes and deck of the
veffel into the water.   There are feveral living witneffes of this fcene.

—How many fwallowed by the waves of the Wallabout—God only knows. Their names, and their individual fufferings are buried with them in oblivion: but their memory fhall be cherifhed as long as liberty endures; and the monument here to be erected fhall tell fucceeding generations the inhuman deeds of former times, that fwept away a countlefs number of the fons of freedom, becaufe they would not be the flaves of defpotifm.

Dreadful, beyond defcription, was the condition of thefe unfortunate prifoners of war. Their fufferings and their forrows were great, and unbounded was their fortitude. Under every privation and every anguifh of life, they firmly encountered the terrors of death, rather than defert the caufe of their country. There, on yonder wave, fwam the black hulk of the Jerfey Prifon Ship; furrounded with 'a clofe incumbent cloud' of peftilence—filled with foul and fuffocating vapours—and echoing with the cries, and the groans, and the supplications of distress. Like a huge monster of the deep, she devoured her thousands at a meal, and as rapidly disgorged the half-consumed and mangled carcasses. There, in her putrefactive bowels, wallowed in filth a croud of living men, amongst the dying and the dead— There the sun-beam never entered, and the zephyr never blew—There was no morsel of wholesome food, nor one drop of pure water. In these black abodes of wretchedness and woe, the grief worn prisoner lay, without a bed to rest his weary limbs, without a pillow to support his aching head—the tattered garment torn from his meagre frame, and vermin preying on his flesh— his food was carrion, and his drink foul as the bilge-water—there was no balm for his wounds, no cordial to revive his fainting spirits, no friend to comfort his heart, nor the soft hand of affec- tion to close his dying eyes—Heaped amongst the dead, while yet the fpark of life lingered in his frame, and hurried to the grave before the cold arms of death had embraced him—O my God! how unutterable was the forrow, and the anguifh of his foul!*

'But,' you will afk, 'was there no relief for thefe victims of mifery?'—No—there was no relief—their aftonifhing fufferings were concealed from the view of the world—and it was only from the few witneffes of the fcene who afterwards lived to tell the cruelties they had endured, that our country became acquainted with their deplorable condition. The grim fentinels, faithful to their charge as the fiends of the nether world, barred the doors againft the hand of charity, and godlike benevolence never entered there—compaffion had

* There is no exaggeration in this defcription, but on the contrary a ftrict adherence to truth.

See *Coffin's Account of the Prifon Ships.*

fled from these manſions of deſpair, and pity wept over other woes.*

* The eſtabliſhing of Priſon Ships will be an everlaſting diſhonour to this war. The Jerſey was a very large and roomy veſſel; ſhe had once carried ſeventy-four guns, but was now ſtripped of everything warlike, and reduced to a naked hulk. All her ports were cloſe ſhut and ſecured, which effectually prevented any current of freſh air between decks, where the priſoners were all ſhut down from ſun-ſet to ſun-riſe, and, during theſe melancholy hours, all acceſs to, or intercourſe with the upper deck, was prohibited. *She had a guard on board, which were forbidden, on pain of ſevere puniſhment, to relieve the wants of any diſtreſſed priſoner;* and was anchored in a ſolitary nook, called the Wallabout, where, at low water, her rotten remains are ſtill to be ſeen, and was made to be, not only the dungeon, but the death of many brave men.

There were confined at this time, in this much-dreaded hulk, about eleven hundred priſoners. No berths were conſtructed for them to lie down in, nor a bench to ſit upon. Many were almoſt without clothes. The dyſentery, fever, phrenzy, and deſpair, prevailed among them, and filled the place with filth, diſguſt, and horror. The ſcantineſs of the allowance, the bad quality of the proviſions, the brutality of the guards, and the ſick, pining for comforts they could not obtain, altogether furniſhed continually one of the greateſt ſcenes of human diſtreſs and miſery ever beheld. It was now the middle of October, and the weather was cool and dry, with froſty nights, ſo that the number of deaths per day were reduced, while Captain Talbot was on

'But,' you will afk again, 'was there no means of efcape from thefe habitations of diftrefs?'—No—there was no efcape except in death, or in that which, to freemen, was worfe than death—the fervice of the enemy. So zealous were the brutal guards, that when the gafping croud below approached the grates and bars to catch the paffing breeze, they met the bayonet's plunge,* and in

board, to an average of *ten*; and this number was confidered by the furvivors but a fmall one, when compared with the terrible mortality that had prevailed in the fhip for three months before. The human bones and fkulls yet bleaching on the fhore of Long-Ifland, and daily expofed by the falling down of the high bank on which the prifoners were buried, is a fhocking fight, and manifeftly demonftrates that the *Jerfey Prifon Ship* had been as deftructive as a field of battle.

Life of Talbot, p. 106.

* I William Burke, a native of Newport, in the ftate of Delaware, was a prifoner on board the fhip Jerfey at the Wallabout, during the Revolution, where I remained in the whole about fourteen months, and during that time, among other cruelties which were committed, I have known many of the American prifoners put to death by the bayonet: in particular I well recollect, that it was the cuftom on board the fhip for but one prifoner at a time

this way numbers were daily delivered from their fufferings by death. Few could ever gain their liberty by being exchanged; and to the immortal honour of thefe patriotic Americans, there is but one inftance on record of a prifoner who accepted the repeated offers of the enemy to enter into their fervice, and when he left his brave companions their dungeon rang with execrations on his head. This indeed was the chief glory of thefe

---

to be admitted on deck at night, befides the guards or fentinels. One night, while the prifoners were many of them affembled at the grate at the hatchway, for the purpofe of obtaining frefh air, and waiting their turn to go on deck, one of the fentinels thruft his bayonet down among them, and in the morning twenty-five of them were found wounded, and ftuck in the head, and dead of the wounds they had thus received. I further recollect that this was the cafe feveral mornings, when fometimes five, fometimes fix, and fometimes eight or ten were found dead by the fame means.

his
WILLIAM ·J· BURKE.
mark

Witnefs,

ISAAC SHERWOOD.

New-York, May 22, 1808.

19

martyrs to liberty, that no rewards nor punifh-
ments could move them to betray their country.
Firm in their purpofe, as the everlafting hills,
and true to the caufe of freedom, they might be
deftroyed—but they could never be enflaved!

You have heard much, fellow-citizens, of the
deeds of the valiant who have fallen, covered
with glory, on the field of battle—you have ad-
mired the intrepidity with which they rufhed
upon the foe, and met a bloody death:—But
here we have examples of fuperior courage, and
more heroic fortitude; for when the combat
waxes hot, amidft the rattle of the drum, and the
thunder of the battle, cowards will be brave—but
to endure the lingering torments of a doleful
prifon—to be wafted away by corroding grief—to
have one's vitals torn by the perpetual gnawings
of hunger—to be confumed by burning thirft—
to be devoured piece-meal by famine, peftilence
and death—oh! this can fubdue a foul of iron,

and make even the brave man a coward.—And yet it fhook not the fortitude of the American prifoner—it moved not his mighty foul!

Was there then no fource of confolation, no ray of comfort in the midft of all their fufferings and all their pains?—Yes, my countrymen,—they felt thofe confolations and comforts which the flave never feels, and which the inexorable vengeance of tyrants can never deftroy—the *love* of country, and the *hope* of immortality: thefe fupported them in their agonies, and raifed them fuperior to the ills of life—without thefe their prifon had been in very deed a hell! But now, from the deep receffes of an enemy's dungeon they could exclaim triumphantly—" *Our country's liberty is dear to our fouls—it deferves a mighty facrifice—let our country be free, and our blood fhall be avenged; it is for that we fuffer—it is for that we die—and as for thefe mortal bodies, and thefe immortal fpirits—O God! O God!—there is another and a better world!'* "

Over such a scene as this, the justice and the vengeance of heaven slept not. There were extraordinary instances of retribution for individual sufferings, and of atonement for national wrongs! You remember the pathetic history of the " two " young brothers belonging to a rifle corps, who " were made prisoners, and sent together on board " the JERSEY. The elder took a fever, and in a " few days became delirious. One night (his end " was fast approaching) he became calm and " sensible, and lamenting his hard fate, and the " absence of his beloved mother, begged for a " little water. His brother, with tears, intreated " the guard to give him some, but in vain. The " sick youth was soon in his last struggles. The " other, in his distress, offered the guard a guinea " for an inch of candle, only that he might see " him die ; and even this was refused !—' *Now,*' " said the surviver, drying up his tears, ' *if it* " *please God I ever regain my liberty, I will be a*

" *most bitter enemy!*'—This awful appeal was not
" in vain. He regained his liberty—he rejoined
" the army—and when the war ended,"* the
blood of one hundred and thirty-five merce-
naries of the enemy had expiated their favage
cruelty!

But, fellow citizens, a more noble vengeance
hath been given to the American nation, in the
acquifition of their Independence. If you had
flain thoufands and tens of thoufands of the Britifh
troops, it would have been felt lefs than your fep-
aration from their power, and your enjoyment of
liberty. It is this that hath remunerated you for
all your fufferings and all your facrifices.—Oh! it
is the beft gift of heaven—prize it as you prize
your life—and magnanimoufly forgive the enor-
mities of a vanquifhed foe!

Say, fellow citizens, is there in the intellectual
or natural world, a more rapturous object of

* Med. Repof. Hex. ii. vol. 3. p. 72.

contemplation than that of a whole people breaking the chains of defpotifm; affuming the 'port
and majefty' of freedom, and taking their ftation
among the nations of the globe. Recollect the
glorious deliverance of ancient Rome from the
grafp of tyranny, and then "look abroad through
"nature, to the range of plants, funs and ada-
"mantine fpheres, wheeling through the void
"immenfe; and fpeak, O man! does this capa-
"cious fcene, with half that kindling majefty
"dilate thy ftrong conception, as when Brutus
"rofe refulgent from the ftroke of Cæfar's fate,
"amidft a crowd of patriots, and his arm aloft
"extending, like eternal Jove when guilt brings
"down the thunder, called aloud on Tully's
"name, and fhook his crimfon fteel, and bade
"the father of his country hail! for lo! the
"tyrant proftrate in the duft, and Rome again
"is free!"*

* Akenfide's Pleafures of the Imagination.

Seeing then how glorious is our liberty, and how dearly it was purchafed by the blood and fufferings of our citizens, let us not forget to reverence the memory of the patriotic dead—let us entomb their afhes with all the honours they fo richly merit. And now, my countrymen, here prefent, will ye not all unite to execute this facred office of affection to the brave who fell for freedom?—By this awful view of death, ye are admonifhed that ye alfo are the fubjects of mortality. Before the lapfe of many years, this vaft affemblage of the living, fhall all be numbered with the dead. Are ye then willing that your bodies, like thefe bodies, fhould be fcattered on the highways, and your flefh devoured by the dogs?—No—humanity revolts at the thought! Go then, and do unto the dead, as ye wifh the living to do unto you, when ye pay the laft debt to nature.

Say, ye bold and generous mariners, who ride

upon the wave and defy the tempeſt, are ye willing when the flag of your country is ſtruck, and
ye periſh in the dungeons of a Priſon Ship, are
ye willing to be denied even a watery grave?—
No—humanity revolts at the thought!—Go
then, and do ye unto the dead, as ye wiſh the
living to do unto you, when ye pay the laſt debt
to nature.

Say, ye martial bands, arrayed in the armour
of war, and decorated with the enſigns of liberty,
when ye fall in defence of your country, are ye
willing that your bodies ſhould rot on the field
of battle, and fatten the paſtures of your native
land?—No—humanity revolts at the thought!—
Go then, and do ye alſo unto the dead, as ye
wiſh the living to do unto you, when ye pay the
laſt debt to nature.

And ye patriotic Sons of Tammany, what ſay
ye of this mournful ſcene?—When ye unbury
the tomahawk to maintain your rights, and die

in the conteft, arc ye willing that the wolf fhould
drink your blood, and the tyger gnaw your
bones?—No—humanity revolts at the thought.
—Go then, and do unto the dead, as ye wifh the
living to do unto you, when ye pay the laft debt
to nature—go, and bury the remains of your
departed brothers.——But ye have already gone
to perform the facred duty; ye have gathered
together all the remnants of their mortal bodies,
that devouring time hath left. Long have ye
defired that they fhould reft in the tombs of
their native land—often have ye dropt the tear
of gratitude to their memory—and now have ye
prepared a fpacious manfion to receive them.
As they were victims of one common fate in life,
one common grave fhall be their lot in death.
There fhall they fweetly fleep together, until the
great day of final retribution, when the Archangel
of heaven fhall proclaim, that 'time fhall be no
more!' "

FTER the Oration, the coffins were depofited in the tomb, and the Proceffion returned to Brooklyn ferry, from whence its paffage to the city was pleafant and expeditious. It was there formed again, and proceeded to the Park, where a circle was formed; the Car of Liberty, and the Stand-ards of the different Societies were placed in the centre, and an air from the band was performed; after which, by a fignal from the Grand Marfhal, the Proceffion was difmiffed.

Thus ended the folemnities of a Funeral Pro-ceffion which had excited more intereft than any other that has ever taken place in America—and not a fingle unfortunate accident happened during the vaft bufinefs of the day. The pious tribute of the living to the dead is always folemn and affecting: a Society in mourning for a hero, is interefting to every one who beholds it: but a nation of freemen, bending in tears over the tomb of *eleven thoufand* martyrs to the caufe of liberty, is a fight never before exhibited, and prefents a fublime theme for the hiftorian and the poet. Happy, happy Columbia! may returning years ftill find thee as thou art this day—*grateful to thy heroes—the nurfe of liberty—at peace with the world!*

APPENDIX.

S elsewhere stated (*Note* 3), the first public movement which was made towards providing a proper place of sepulture for the remains of the Prison Ship dead, was by the town of Brooklyn, in the years 1792 and 1793. Their well-meant efforts, however, were defeated by the refusal of Mr. Jackson to deliver the sacred deposits into their keeping, and the matter subsequently came into the hands of the Order of St. Tammany. The grand ceremonial with which that Society inaugurated their

propofed undertaking, is fully recorded in the work which we have here reprinted; but the refults, or rather the lack of refults, of this aufpicious beginning, form a chapter, which, although not creditable to American patriotifm, may be added as an appendix to this " Hiftorical Account."

For awhile, after the temporary interment of the bones of the Martyrs, there feemed no doubt that a nation's gratitude would be converted into the gold which fhould build their monument. Tammany Hall flamed with excitement. Committees were appointed to collect money, individuals proffered donations, the State itfelf contributed one thoufand dollars. But all this fervid excitement foon collapfed. Tammany Hall, good at the beginning, did not keep up the ftimulus. Some money was collected, but fcattered—no one knew or cared where—private donations were not called for, and the fum appropriated by the State was finally returned to the State treafury, to be realized, it is hoped, with increafe, at fome future day, when the patriotifm of our people fhall finally make amends for the long delay of the paft.

So the bubble burft—the tide of population fo furged in upon this favored region of Brooklyn, that the old elements were diffolved in the current of new comers, and the very purpofe of this vault and its wooden covering were well-nigh forgotten. In courfe of time, by an alteration of the grade of Jackfon ftreet, the walls of the vault were infringed upon—and finally, the very lot on which it ftood was *fold for taxes!* Then BENJAMIN ROMAINE, the treafurer of the fund of 1808—a true patriot, and fully earneft in his efforts to fecure a monument—came forward and bought it. He had been himfelf a fufferer by imprifonment in the old Sugar-Houfe Prifon at New York, and he now took pleasure in rescuing from desecration the remains of those whose sufferings he had shared, and whose memory he revered. He erected an ante-chamber over the vault, and other appropriate adornments and inscriptions.*

The better to prevent any further desecration

---

* These improvements, etc., are thus fully described in a little pamphlet published by him on the 4th of July, 1839:

"The following inscriptions are now displayed in and about the sacred premises:

"*First*. The PORTAL to the TOMB of 11,500 patriot prisoners of War, who died in dungeons and pestilential Prison Ships, in and about the City of New-York, during the War of our Revolution. The top is capt with two large Urns, in black, and a white Globe in the centre.

"*Second*. The interior of the Tomb contains thirteen Coffins, arranged in the order as observed in the Declaration of Independence, and inserted thus —*New Hampshire, Massachusetts, Rhode Island, Connecticut, New-York, New-Jersey, Pennsylvania, Delaware, Maryland, Virginia, North Carolina, South Carolina*, and *Georgia*.

"*Third*. Thirteen beautifully turned posts, painted white, each capt with a small Urn, in black; and between the posts, the above-named States are fully lettered.

"*Fourth*. In 1778 the Colonial Congress promulgated the Federal-league

of this, to him, hallowed fpot, Mr. Romaine appropriated the tomb as a burial-place for himfelf
and his family, and with that intent, placed there,

Compact, though it was not finally ratified until 1781, only two years before
the Peace of 1783.

"*Fifth.* In 1789 our grand national Convention, "*to form a more perfect
Union,*" did ordain "*the prefent Conftitution for the United States of America,*"
to be ONE ENTIRE SOVEREIGNTY, and in ftrict adhefion to the equally neceffary and facred STATE RIGHTS. Such a Republic muft endure forever!!!

"*Sixth.* In the fame year. 1789, in the City of New-York, Wafhington
began the firft Prefidential career. The wide-fpread Eagle of Union, with
a gilded Sun and Star in his beak, and ftanding erect on a Globe, is now
reprefented as waiting on Wafhington's command, and then as inftantly raifing his flight in the heavens,—and like the Orb of Day, fpeedily became
vifible to half the Globe. Wafhington had appeared, uncovered, before the
majefty of the people, under the canopy, in front of our City Hall, when
Chancellor Livingfton adminiftered to him the oath of office, and then proclaimed, LONG LIVE GEORGE WASHINGTON! The air was rent with fhouts
of acclamation, and our goodly fhip Union moved on our ways, a model for
the Univerfe!!—A witnefs to this fcene declared that it appeared to him
that the hofts of heaven, at that moment, were looking down with approbation on the act. That he was deprived of utterance, and could only wave
his hat among the multitude!—I was alfo a witnefs to the fcene!—Then it
was, *at that moment,* when our State Sovereignties, not our equally facred

21

many years before his death, the coffin in which he fhould be interred.

The interior of the tomb, at this time, has thus been well defcribed by an old refident of Brooklyn.*

STATE RIGHTS, ceafed to exift, and the Sovereign power was proclaimed to be invefted *in the whole people of the United States,* ONE AND INDIVISIBLE!!!

"*Seventh.* The Conftitution of the United States confifts of TWO PARTS —the SUPREME SOVEREIGNTY, and the unadulterated STATE RIGHTS, one and infeparable. It has no parallel except the facred Decalogue by Mofes, which proclaimed our duties to God and man, *one and indivifible,*—fix thoufand years ago.

"*Eighth.* In the ante-chamber to the Tomb will be arranged the Bufts, or other infignia, of the moft diftinguifhed deceafed Military men and Civilians of the Revolution. The Governors and Legiflatures of the Old Thirteen States, will confer a great favour by fending them to Benjamin Romaine, No. 21 Hudfon Street, City of New-York."—*Review. The Tomb of the Martyrs, adjoining the United States Navy-Yard, Brooklyn City, in Jackfon Street, who died in dungeons and peftilential Prifon Ships, in and about the City of New-York, during the feven years of our Revolutionary War. By Benjamin Romaine, an old native citizen of New-York. New-York: Printed by C. C. & E. Childs, Jr., 80 Vefey Street, 4th July, 1839. 8vo., pp. 7, and lithographic view of Tomb, from which our frontifpiece is copied.*

* Once-a-Week, Feb. 6, 1864.

"One Saturday, of fchool-boy leifure for that "mifchief" which Satan finds for "idle hands to do," I determined to penetrate the depth of this tomb, and fought the building, fully bent on gaining the interior, and knowing all that could be revealed to the aftonifhed eye. This was not very difficult—the faftenings were loofe, and after fome little toil the exterior door fwung open, and revealed a fort of veftibule, in which were a few plafter bufts of diftinguifhed heroes, covered with the incruftations of dampnefs and neglect. There were fteps leading below into a vault. Thefe I fearlefsly defcended, and then ftood entranced and nearly paralyzed by a fenfe of awe which has not left me to this day. Standing, chiefly in perpendicular pofition, around the vault, were thirteen immenfe coffins, each having thereon the name of one of the thirteen original States. I could fee enough through interftices to fhow me that thefe were filled with

bones, and I knew I was ftanding in the midft
of that noble army of martyrs whofe blood had
gone up as a holy and acceptable facrifice on the
altar of American Freedom. I have felt the
thrill of other altar places ; have felt deep emo-
tions at the grave, and fublime fenfations upon
the mountain tops, but I am very fure that on
no other occafion did I ever feel my whole nature fo elevated to a fenfe of majeftic reverence, as
in the prefence of that fublime and filent company.

" Refting on one or two of the coffins which
were laid horizontally, was one fmaller coffin of
the ordinary fize of one individual. This was
vacant, but had upon its lid the name of ' Benjamin Romaine,' as if it was intended that fome
perfon of this name yet walking among the lilli-
putians of the earth fhould, in his duft, be
placed here, to lie among thefe giant patriots,
fecure, if with them forgotten upon earth, to
rife with them hereafter."

And there, in that vault, and in the coffin fo long and fo reverently prepared, was buried Benjamin Romaine (at his death in 1844, at the age of 82), fit fentinel of that group, who performed deeds of heroic facrifice, the worthieft which pen, pencil, and monument can celebrate.

Two years before his death, however, in the year 1842, the citizens of Brooklyn, through a highly refpectable committee, petitioned the Legiflature for leave to remove the bones, for the purpofe of appropriate fepulture. Againft this Mr. Romaine remonftrated. He faid:

" I have guarded thefe facred remains with a reverence, which perhaps, at this day, all may not appreciate or feel, for more than thirty years. They are now in their right place, near the Wallabout, and adjoining the Navy-Yard. They are my property. I have expended more than nine hundred dollars in and about their protection and prefervation. *I commend them to*

the protection of the general government. I be-
queath them to my country. This concern is very
facred to me. It lies near my heart. I fuffered
with thofe whofe bones I venerate. I fought
befide them—I bled with them."

In confequence of this remonftrance nothing
was then done.

But after the old man had paffed away, in the
year 1845, public attention was again called to
the neglected condition of thefe remains, and the
matter was alfo brought to the attention of the
National Congrefs by a Report introduced by
the Military Committee to the Houfe of Reprefentatives,* recommending an appropriation of
$20,000 for the purpofe of affording a fecure
tomb and fitting monument to the Martyrs.
This alfo failed of its object, and the matter flept
for ten years. At the expiration of that period, in

---

* This Report, drawn up by the Hon. Henry C. Murphy, of Brooklyn,
forms Document No. 176, Rep. of Ho. of Reps., 1844–45.

1855, a large and influential meeting of the citizens of Brooklyn was held, at which it was refolved, " that the time has arrived when the Cities of New-York and Brooklyn cannot, without criminality, longer delay the neceffary efforts for rearing the Monument to the Martyrs of the Prifon Ships," and an organization was formed for the purpofe, entitled "THE MARTYRS' MONUMENT ASSOCIATION," in which each Senatorial Diftrict in the State of New-York, and each State and Territory, is reprefented. They fet to work with commendable accuracy, felected a fitting fite—the lofty fummit of Fort Greene—fecured plans for the propofed monument, agitated the fubject publicly and privately, folicited donations, etc., etc., and "yet there is no monument! no ftone bearing the record of their patriotic devotion to principle, and their more than heroic death."

We underftand that the " Martyrs Affociation" ftill entertain hopes of ultimately fecuring

their object, and that they have made progrefs in
their endeavors; that an appropriate lot of land
on Fort Greene, or Wafhington Park, has been
granted by the Common Council of the City of
Brooklyn; and, furely, we may hope that this
attempt to honor the memory of the dead heroes
will not prove abortive, as its predeceffors have
done.

To the citizens of New-York and Brooklyn
are peculiarly appropriate thofe folemn words of
an ancient patriot, under circumftances not un-
like our own—"Oh, my countrymen! thefe
dead bodies afk no monument. Their monument arofe when they fell, and as long as liberty
fhall have defenders, their names will be imperifh-
able. But, oh, my countrymen, it is *we* who
need a monument to their honor; *we,* who furvive, not having yet proved that we, too, could
die for our country and be immortal. *We* need
a monument, that the widows and children of

the dead, and the whole country, and the ſhades
of the departed, and all future ages, may ſee and
know that we honor patriotiſm, and virtue, and
liberty, and truth; for next to performing a
great deed, and achieving a noble character, is to
honor ſuch characters and deeds."

22

NOTES.

(I.) The WALLABOUT, is the name applied to the bay, or cove, now occupied, in part, by the U. S. Navy-Yard at Brooklyn. The word Wallabout is a corruption of the old Holland words " Waal" and " boght," and has generally been fuppofed to have been applied to this locality, on account of its having been originally fettled by fome of the Walloon families, who emigrated to the New Netherlands. This point, however, has recently been queftioned by fome of the local antiquarians of Brooklyn, who claim that the firft fettlers of this portion of the town, were not exclufively Walloons, but were moftly of mixed defcent, Norwegian, Italian, French, Dutch, &c. ; and that the term Wallabout may be more properly derived from another fignification of

" Waal," viz., *a bay*, and "boght," *a bend, i. e.* "the bend of the bay," an apt defcription of the locality. As " Waal" alfo means "*a Whale*"—it may be that the true tranfla-tion of the name fhould be "*the Whale's bay*"—poffibly from the firanding or killing of one of thofe animals in that locality. Such a circumftance, although of rare occurrence, is by no means impoffible, and would have been of fufficient importance to give a name to the place where it happened.

The Indian name of the Wallabout was *Mercyckawick*, or " the fandy place ;" from *me*, the article in the Algonquin dialect ; *reckwa*, fand ; and *ick*, locality. The name was probably applied at firft to the bottom land, or beach ; and what is now Wallabout bay, was formerly called " The boght of Mareckawick." The Indians who inhabited that part of t he prefent city of Brooklyn, derived their tribal name from this bay.

(2.) This eftimate of 11,000, or, as elfewhere fiated, 11,500, whether correct or not, undoubtedly originated in the following newfpaper paragraph :

Fifhkill, May 8, '83.

TO ALL PRINTERS OF PUBLIC NEWSPAPERS.

Tell it to the world, and let it be publifhed in every

Newspaper throughout America, Europe, Asia and Africa, to
the everlasting disgrace and infamy of the British King's commanders at New York : That during the late war, it is said,
11,644 American prisoners have suffered death by their inhuman, cruel, savage and barbarous usage on board the filthy
and malignant British Prison Ship, called the Jersey, lying at
N. Y.   Britons, tremble, lest the vengeance of Heaven fall
on your isle, for the blood of these unfortunate victims.

AN AMERICAN.

(3.) JOHN JACKSON was a native of Jerusalem, Queens
Co., L. I., whence he removed with his brothers Samuel and
Treadwell, to the village of Brooklyn, shortly after the close
of the Revolution.   It is probable that the brothers were
possessed of some means, for they soon purchased large estates
in Brooklyn, which could, at that early period, be had at
very low prices.   John Jackson, about 1791, purchased the
large and valuable farm then known as the " Remsen Estate,"
situated on the Wallabout, and comprising about thirty acres
of land, and thirty-five acres of pond, together with the old mill
and dwelling-house—for which he paid the sum of $17,000.
It was in making improvements on this farm that public
attention seems first to have been attracted, by the disinter-
ment of the remains of those buried from the Prison Ships—
large quantities of bones being found in cutting away the

high banks, which then formed the ſhore of the Bay. In the year 1801, Mr. Jackſon ſold to the United States, for the ſum of $40,000, (through Francis Childs, a middleman,) forty acres of this property, which has ever ſince been occupied by the Government as a Navy-Yard. About this time, alſo, the ſuppreſſion of the Rebellion in Ireland cauſed the emigration to this country of many perſons who had been engaged in that unfortunate ſtruggle; and a portion of theſe refugees, who had a little property, were induced to purchaſe lots on Jackſon's land, at a ſpot, to which—cleverly appealing to their patriotiſm—he had given the name of " Vinegar Hill," in honor of the ſcene of the laſt conflict of that memorable rebellion. The ſpeculative turn of Mr. Jackſon's character is alſo exhibited in his gift to the Tammany Society of land in the Wallabout, for the purpoſe of erecting a monument to the Martyrs. Being a prominent politician, and a Sachem of the Tammany Society, he undoubtedly conceived the idea of turning to a political uſe, and to his perſonal aggrandizement, the large depoſit of Priſon Ship remains of which he had thus accidentally become the poſſeſſor. That we do not unjuſtly eſtimate his real motives in this tranſaction is evident, we think, from the following facts. In 1792, the citizens of the town of Brooklyn, at an annual Town Meeting, reſolved that the bones, difinterred and collected by Mr. Jackfon, fhould be removed to and buried in the grave-yard of the Reformed Dutch Church, and a monument erected over them. A Committee, of which Gen. Jeremiah Johnfon was Chairman, was appointed to carry the refolution into effect, but upon their application, in 1793, Mr. Jackfon refufed to yield up the cuftody of the remains; and it was referved for St. Tammany's followers to make them the opportune caufe of a magnificent ceremonial, as grand in its promifes, as it was empty in refults. Mr. Jackfon certainly appears in Brooklyn hiftory moftly in the character of a fhrewd fpeculator,—as the originator and Prefident of the Wallabout Bridge Company,— as the builder of a faw-mill on the adjoining meadow, to be moved by wind, which failed,—as the vendor of a part of the fame meadow, (to Capt. Ifaac Chauncey, of the U. S. N.) for the purpofe of erecting thereon powder magazines, but the dampnefs of the place damaged the powder, and, confequently, the reputation of the magazines. Indeed, in his fale of land and water privilege to the United States for a Navy-Yard, he feems to have granted rather more of the mill-ftream than his own title fairly included, and to have covered the excefs by an ambiguoufly-worded deed, which ultimately gave rife to fome well-founded complaint on the part of the citizens of the town—to which the faid water privilege belonged; and to an extenfive correfpondence between them and the Secretary of the Navy.

Mr. Jackfon is defcribed, by thofe who knew him, as a large man, of coarfe features and florid complexion, loud fpoken, energetic in his movements, and an ardent politician. His domeftic relations were notorioufly unhappy; and he was always involved in petty law difficulties, owing to his reluctance in paying his debts, without being obliged, as he felicitoufly expreffed it, "to take a receipt, according to law, on the back of a conftable's execution."

(4.) The TAMMANY SOCIETY, or *Columbian Order*, was formed in 1789, by one William Mooney, an upholfterer, and refident of New York during Wafhington's adminiftration. It derived its name from that of the celebrated Delaware Indian chief Tamanund, whofe attachment to liberty was greater than his love of life. It claims to have been " founded on the true and genuine principles of republicanifm, and holds out as its objects, the fmile of charity, the chain of friendfhip, and the flame of liberty; and, in general, whatever may tend to perpetuate the *love of freedom*, or the political advantages of this Country."

Its Officers are a Grand Sachem, thirteen Sachems (in allusion to the Old Thirteen States), and a Grand Council, of which the Sachems are members. " Tammany was," says Hammond,* " at first so popular, that most persons of merit became members; and so numerous were they that its anniverfary (12th of May) was regarded as a holiday. At that time, there were no party politics mixed up in its proceedings. But when President Washington rebuked ' self-created focieties,' from an apprehenfion that their ultimate tendency would be hostile to the public tranquillity, the members of Tammany suppofing their institution to be included in the reproof, nearly all left it. The founder (Grand Sachem Mooney), and a few others, continued steadfast, and from this time it became a political institution, and took ground with Jefferson. It continued to increafe in members, and made a great rally, about 1812, in fupport of President Madifon's administration, and to fecure his re-election in that year. The fociety has been continued to the prefent time, folely as a political organization."

Their original head-quarters were at Martling's Long Room, on the corner of Naffau and Spruce streets, the pref-

* Hammond's Political Hist. New York.

23

ent fite of the Tract Society's Building. In 1809, they paffed a
"Law" for the "building of a Wigwam," and a Committee
of thirteen was appointed to carry it into effect. The fpot
felected, was on the corner of Chatham and Frankfort ftreets,
where, on the 13th of May, 1811, the 22d Anniverfary of the
Society, the corner-ftone was laid with great ceremony by
Clarkfon Crolius, and an oration was pronounced by Alpheus
Sherman. The building thus commenced, has continued to
the prefent day to be the rallying point of the New York
Democracy. During the conteft between Clinton and
Tompkins, in the earlier part of the prefent century,
the Tammany Society efpoufed the caufe of the latter,
and became thenceforth ftrongly "Anti-Clintonite." In
this connection, it will be proper to notice the celebrated
toaft offered by Gen. Jackfon, at a reception dinner given to
him by the Tammany Society, on his vifit to New York in
1819. This toaft, "De Witt Clinton, the enlightened
Statefman, and Governor of the great and patriotic State of
New-York,"—produced an excitement at the time almoft
equal to that which would have followed the explofion of a
bomb-fhell in the midft of the feftive board; and which can
fcarcely be underftood by any one not thoroughly verfed in
"that moft unfathomable of fubjects, the Politics of the State

of New-York." It is needlefs to fay that the lion-hearted old General was by no means ignorant of the "ins and outs" of New York local politics, or of the unpalatable nature of his toaſt to the "Bucktails" in the halls of St. Tammany.

It will be interefting to our readers to know the compofi-tion of the Society in the year 1809, as exhibited in the New York Directory of that year:

Benjamin Romaine, *Grand Sachem*—William Mooney, *Father of the Council*—William I. Waldron, *Treafurer*—Jonas Humbert, *Secretary*—Abraham O. Valentine, *Saga-more*—William Mooney, *Sachem of the New York, or Eagle tribe, and Father of the Council*—William Jones, *Sachem of the New Hampſhire, or Otter tribe*—John Forbes, *Sachem of the Maſſachufetts, or Panther tribe*—John Hopper, *Sachem of the Rhode Iſland, or Beaver tribe*—William Peterſon, *Sachem of the Connecticut, or Bear tribe*—John Striker, *Sachem of the New Jerfey, or Tortoife tribe*—Benjamin Aycrigg, *Sachem of the Pennfylvania, or Rattle-Snake tribe*—Judah Hammond, *Sachem of the Delaware, or Tiger tribe*—Napthali Judah, *Sachem of the Maryland, or Fox tribe*—Ifrael Titus, *Sachem of the Virginia, or Deer tribe*—Samuel Cowdry, *Sachem of the North Carolina, or Buffalo tribe*—Stephen Bourdett, *Sachem of the South Carolina, or Raccoon*

tribe—John P. Haff, *Sachem of the Georgia, or Wolf tribe*—
Henry Howard, *Scribe to the Council*— —— Roome, *Wiſkin-
kie.*

In this connection we prefent to our readers the following
and interefting letter, from Dr. Samuel L. Mitchell, LL. D.,
the original of which is in the Library of the Long Ifland
Hiftorical Society. It was addreffed to B. F. Thompfon,
Efq., the Hiftorian of Long Ifland.

New-York, Aug. 9, 1811.

MY DEAR SIR,

I thank you for your ingenious and patriotic oration to the
Columbian Order, for our laft National New-Year's day. I
fhall preferve it among the mementoes of my valued acquaintance.

If I can find anywhere a copy of my long talk "on the
life, exploits and precepts of Tammany," I will certainly
fend it to you. The only copy that I have is bound up with
various other pamphlets, and very inconvenient to be fent
abroad. It is a large octavo volume. The Society gave the
orator but a few copies; and they were begged away by
parents, who wifhed to read to their children, the advice
given by Tammany to the tribes of his people. Buel, the
printer, who publifhed it, is fince dead; and I know not
who purchafed his ftock. I wifh, with all my heart, I could
get a copy for you.

It was a fportive thing; done during a time when I had

inflamed eyes, and could not bear the light; at a period, too, when political fervour was very hot, juft when Mr. Jay had fucceeded in his election as Governor of the State. I intended the compofition to be a fort of moral romance; yet what was my furprife to find it confidered by both political parties, a deep Political Allegory! The Democrats on one fide, and the Federalifts on the other, difcovered manifold meanings that had never occurred to me, and their refpective fignifications were as oppofite as their ways of thinking.

One thing remarkable grew out of my Tammanial addrefs. A copy by fome means fell into the hands of the Earl of Buchan. He prefented it to the Society of Scottifh Anti-quaries; and I fhortly after received a certificate from Edinburgh, of having been elected a member. So much for our fredifh Saint and Sage. It will be gratifying to me to receive your Effay on Tobacco; though I am fomewhat a fmoker of cigars myfelf. I am fatisfied I fhall read it with fatisfaction, altho' Sir J. Sinclair has proved that the mod-erate ufe of it does not fhorten life an hour. Truly and with much efteem,

Yours,

SAM. L. MITCHELL.

With the Tammany Society, alfo, originated the " Ameri-can Mufeum," which has for many years been fo prominent an inftitution of New York City. This appears from a cir-cular, dated May 1, 1791, headed " AMERICAN MUSEUM, under the patronage of the Tammany Society, or Columbian

Order." To the ufe of this enterprife the Corporation granted a room in the City Hall, to be open on Fridays, and articles fent there, or to Mr. John Pintard, No. 57 King Street, would be "thankfully accepted." Pintard was the Secretary, and Gardner Baker its keeper. It was fuccefsful for many years, and, in 1808, became the property of Baker, and was known as "Baker's American Mufeum." Dr. Scudder afterwards purchafed and kept it in a building in the rear of the City Hall, on the third floor, and it was called "Scudder's American Mufeum." Subfequently it paffed into the ownerfhip of Phineas T. Barnum.

(5.) SAMUEL LATHAM MITCHELL, M. D., LL. D., a diftinguifhed phyfician, naturalift and literary man of his day, was born in North Hempftead, Queen's Co., N. Y., Aug. 20, 1764. After purfuing a thorough claffical and profeffional courfe of ftudy under able inftructors, he availed himfelf of the fuperior advantages of the Univerfity of Edinburgh, in 1783; and upon his return to America, devoted a portion of his leifure to the ftudy of the Law, and the conftitution of this Republic, under the direction of Robert Yates, at that time Chief Juftice of the State of New York. His reputation rapidly culminated, and honors flowed in upon him from every quarter. The Faculty of Columbia College bestowed upon him the degree of Master of Arts. In 1788, he was one of the Commissioners who treated with the Six Nations, and obtained from them the cession of Western New York. Meanwhile, he practiced his profession, and was indefatigable in his study of the natural sciences. In 1790, he was sent to the Legislature of his native State, and, in 1792, was chosen Professor of Chemistry, Natural Sciences and Agriculture, in Columbia College. In 1796, he made his famous report on the mineralogical survey of the State of New York; and the next year, commenced the publication of the "*Medical Repository*," which he edited for sixteen years. He was a member of the Legislature in 1798, when Chancellor Livingston applied for the exclusive right of navigating the Hudson river with boats propelled "by fire, or steam;" and, having presented and carried a bill for that purpose, in spite of opposition and ridicule, had the pleasure of accompanying Fulton, in 1807, on his first voyage in a steamboat. In 1814, he was, with Drs. Williamson and Hosack, a founder of the Literary and Philosophical Society of New York; and with others, in the establishment of the Institution for the Deaf and Dumb. In 1818, he was one of three, who disinterred the remains of a Mastodon, in Orange

County, N. Y., and, in 1819, was a prominent member of
the convention held at Philadelphia, for preparing a National
Pharmacopœia. He was the founder, and for a long time
prefident of the New York Lyceum of Natural Hiſtory, and
a prominent member of the New York Hiſtorical Society.
For twenty years actively engaged as one of the phyſicians of
the New York Hoſpital, in addition to all his other duties,
he found time to mingle in political ſtrife, and ſhare in the
labors and honors of official ſtation. He reprefented the
City of New York, in Congrefs, fix confecutive years,
and was afterwards U. S. Senator, 1804–1810. The
proudeſt day of his life was, perhaps, the 26th of October,
1825, when the Erie Canal Celebration united the waters of
our inland lakes with thoſe of the Atlantic; and crowned
with fuccefs the ſtruggles and influence which he, for many
years, had confecrated to this undertaking. He was poſſeſſed,
in ſhort, of vaſt and varied knowledge; and yet, he fometimes
advanced opinions of which the world had not yet dreamed,
he was fneered at by the fcioliſt, and ridiculed by ſhallow
upſtarts in fcience. He was thoroughly appreciated in
Europe, where almoſt every literary and fcientific inſtitution
ᵗhought it an honor to enrol his name upon its liſt of members. Dr. Mitchell died at his refidence, in New York

City, on the 7th of September, 1831, in the 67th year of his age.

(6.) WILLIAM MOONEY, was an upholſterer, who did buſineſs, in the year 1796, at Nos. 31 and 34 Naſſau ſtreet, and, in 1809, at 76 Maiden lane. He was the founder of the Tammany Society, or Columbian Order, of which he was a Sachem of the New York or Eagle tribe, and in 1792, was one of the Truſtees of the Muſeum founded by that Order, and which has ſince been better known as "Barnum's American Muſeum" (ſee Note 4). In 1808 he was Father of the Council, and at all times a zealous member of "Old Tammany." The following is his advertiſement, as pub-liſhed in *The Argus, or Greenleaf's New Daily Advertiſer,* No. 215, January 15, 1796.

WILLIAM MOONEY,

UPHOLSTERER,

At his Furniture Warehouſe,

No. 31 NASSAU STREET,

HAS FOR SALE, CHEAP,

ONE HUNDRED pair of elegant faſhionable LOOKING GLASSES, in burniſhed gold frames, from 160l. down to 15l. per pair, juſt received.

24

10,000 pieces PAPER HANGINGS, French and Englifh, comprifing the beft and moft elegant affortment in this city; among which are, plain blue, green, yellow, pink, ftraw, and falmon—alfo white, green, blue, and black marble pannel do., a great variety; fome very elegant gold and marble; two fets very beautiful paper for large drawing rooms; cornices and pillars, with ftatues for halls and entries; befides about 200 beautiful figures printed on paper: And Borders of every defcription, in the higheft tafte.

300 French CHAIRS, high, eafy, and neat, in fets; the firft of the kind offered for fale in this city.

Bruffels, Wilton, Mock, Turkey, coach, ingrained, and common CARPETING.

30 pieces HAIR SEATING, ftriped, figured, and plain.

A few fuperb FIGURES for mantle pieces, in porcelain, perhaps the moft exquifite pieces of art and finifhed workmanfhip which have been for fale in this city—Alfo, a few large beautiful JARS.

A few pieces handfome furniture CHINTZES; with a good affortment of excellent FRINGES, of all colors: CORDS, TASSELS, and LACES, juft imported.

A number of large fine rofe BLANKETS; and green and fpotted RUGS.

American BED-TICKEN, manufactured in Beverly, superior to any imported, warranted not to shed feathers.

Flanders BED TICK, India MATS, small patent OIL CLOTHS.

20 large looking glass PLATES; the largest 71 by 36 inches wide.

2 pair very large GERANDOLES.

COTTON COUNTERPAINES.

About 3000 wt. of FEATHERS, various qualities, warranted wholesome.

2 Polonese BED STEADS, with elegant yellow damask curtains complete, made in Paris.

Cabriole and other SOFAS.

Easy and other CHAIRS.

Feather BEDS.

Hair, moss, and common MATTRASSES.

Bed and window CURTAINS, with every article in the UPHOLSTERY line, made in the completest and most fashionable stile.

Paper hangings put up; ship's cabins furnished with curtains, mattrasses, &c.

Orders from any part of the country gratefully received, and punctually and honorably executed.

☞ Wm. Mooney requests the ladies and gentlemen of

this city, as well foreigners as citizens, who have honored him with their commands, to accept his moſt unfeigned thanks for their many and continued favors—He flatters himſelf, from a praĉtical and experimental knowledge of his profeſſion, and the large ſtock of materials he now poſſeſſes, to be able to execute any orders with elegance and diſpatch. He is determined to make his ſtudy to pleaſe, and do juſtice to all.

N. B. Some of the beſt workmen in this country, from Europe, are in his employ.

Dec. 16.   89—d—lf.

(7.) NATHAN SANDFORD, was an attorney and counſellor at law, at 27 Pine ſtreet, dwelling next door, No. 25. He was at one time United States Diſtriĉt Attorney.

(8.) WILLIAM BOYD, was a merchant, at 12 Stone ſtreet, and in 1806, ſenior partner of the firm of Boyd & Suydam, at No. 21 South ſtreet.

(9.) Gen. DAVID WOOSTER, born at Stratford, Ct., March 2, 1710; graduated at Yale in 1738, and the next year was made lieutenant in the Spaniſh War; ſoon after became captain of the colony's coaſt-guard ſhip. Was a captain in Col. Burr's regiment, in the Louiſburg expedition of 1745, and went to Europe in command of a cartel ſhip. Was made a captain in the regular ſervice, under Sir Wm. Pepperell, and was firſt a colonel, and then a brigadier in the Old Seven Years' French War, which ended in 1763. Was one of the principal conſpirators againſt Ticonderoga in 1775, and was appointed one of the eight brigadiers (third in rank) of the newly-organized Continental army. He had the chief command in Canada, for awhile, in 1776, and was then appointed the firſt major-general of the militia, in his native ſtate, where he was mortally wounded, April 27, 1777, in reſiſting Tryon's invaſion, and died at the age of ſixty-ſeven years.

(10.) Gen. Nicholas Herkimer, a gallant officer, of Dutch deſcent, commiſſioned a lieutenant in the Schenectady battalion of militia, in 1758; colonel of the firſt battalion of militia in Herkimer county, in 1775; brigadier-general of the militia of Tryon county, organized by Congreſs, in 1776. Was alſo a member of the Tryon County Committee of Safety, and Chairman *pro tem.*, in 1775. In June 1777, at the head of about 450 local militia, he held an important conference with the Indian chieftain Brant, with a view to secure the neutrality of the Indians in the struggle between England and the Colonies. This attempt, however, proved unsuccessful. He was killed, in 1777, at the battle of Oriskany, while gallantly leading the militia of Tryon county to the assistance of Col. Ganzevoort at Fort Stanwix.

(11.) Gen. WILLIAM DAVIDSON, a native of Pennsylvania, but "raised" in North Carolina; a major of one of the first regiments enlisted in Carolina, but first saw active service in New Jersey. In November, 1779, was detailed to act under Gen. Lincoln in the South; was seriously wounded at Calson's Mills, and after the battle of Camden was made a brigadier-general. Was killed at the action of Cowan's Ford, February 1781. He was a man of pleasing address, great activity and pure devotion.

(12.) Gen. JOSEPH WARREN was born at Roxbury, Mass., in 1740, and graduated at Harvard College in 1759. Became an eminent physician, and a prominent actor in the opening scenes of the American Revolution. He was one of the earliest members of the "Sons of Liberty" in Boston, and a friend and co-laborer with Adams, Otis, and others, in planning measures for resisting the encroachments of British power. When Hancock went to the Continental Congress,

Warren was chofen to fill his place as Prefident of the Provincial Congrefs. That body beftowed upon him the commiffion of major-general, only four days before the memorable battle of Breed's Hill, where he was killed, June 17,
1775.

(13.) Gen. HUGH MERCER, a native of Scotland, was an
affiftant furgeon in the battle of Culloden, and the companion of Wafhington in the Indian wars of 1755 and '56.
He received a medal from the City and Corporation of Philadelphia for his conduct in the Expedition againft the Indian
village of Kittaning. When the Revolution broke out, Dr.
Mercer refided at Frederickfburg, Va., but immediately took
up arms, commanded three regiments of minute men in
1775, and in 1776, drilled and organized large bodies of the
Virginia militia. On the 5th of June, 1776, he received
from Congrefs the commiffion of a brigadier, and on the 3d
of June, 1777, was killed at the battle of Princeton.

(14.) FRANCIS NASH firft diftinguifhed himfelf as a captain in the *Regulator War*, in the year 1771, in the colony
of North Carolina. At the commencement of the Revolution he was made a colonel by the convention of his ftate,

and in February, 1777, was commiffioned a brigadier in the Continental army, and was killed at the battle of German-town the fame year.

(15.) The Baron de Kalb, knight of the royal order of military merit, was a native of Alface, in Germany, and educated in the French army. He came to America in 1777, with General Lafayette, and being a brigadier in the French fervice, was commiffioned as a major-general in the American army, by Congrefs, on the 15th of September of that year. Was actively engaged in various commands, where his high abilities and ripe experience gained the refpect and admiration of all. He fell at the battle of Camden, pierced with eleven wounds, and died three days after, Auguft 16th, 1780.

(16.) In the interim, however, as will be feen by the following ftatement (*Trans. Am. Inflitute*, 1852), the patriotifm of a private individual reproved the hefitation of the Congrefs of a great people.

" A. Chandler, Efq.

" *Dear Sir,*—A fhort time before the death of my mother (Feb., 1844), fhe gave me this paper, and remarked, ' your father and myfelf were walking in the neighborhood where the bones were fcattered over the furface, fome partly and others entirely uncovered. He remarked that it was a difgrace to the country. After walking a little farther, he faid he would have them collected. He left me and went to a neighboring houfe, where he found that there were feveral children. He made this agreement with the father, and under this agreement the bones were collected.

"B. AYCRIGG.

"*New York, Nov.* 28, 1853."

"WALLABOUT, *Long-Ifland, Aug.* 24, 1805.

"I do hereby agree to collect all the human bones as far as may be without digging, about the fhore and banks of this place, (buried from on board the Prifon Ship Jerfey during the Revolution of America,) and deliver the fame to Benjn. Aycrigg, at this place, at one cent per pound, within one year from this date.

"AMOS CHENEY."

Cheney was an Irifhman living in the vicinity.

(17.) JACOB VANDERVOORT was a coachmaker, doing bufinefs at 24 Chambers ftreet, and living at 14 Catherine ftreet.

(18.) ISSACHAR COZZENS, Jr., was a diftiller in Divifion ftreet.

(19.) BURDETT STRYKER, whofe bufinefs was that of a tallow chandler and butcher, refided in Brooklyn. He was a free-hearted, fympathetic man, much noted for his frequent

25

and unobtruſive acts of benevolence—in ſhort, a ſort of "rough diamond."

(20.) ROBERT TOWNSEND, Jun., was a carpenter, at 420 Broadway.

(21.) BENJAMIN WATSON, ſhoemaker, reſided at 89 Chatham ſtreet.

(22.) SAMUEL COWDREY, an attorney at law, reſided at 72 Cherry ſtreet.

(23.) The JERSEY, originally a ſixty-gun ſhip, became unfit for ſervice, and in 1780 was placed in the Wallabout, and uſed as a priſon ſhip until the cloſe of the war, when ſhe was left to decay on the ſpot where her victims had ſuffered. On her quarter-deck was a barricade, ten feet high, with a door and loop-holes on each ſide. The officers' cabin and ſteerage for ſailors were under the quarter-deck. Her crew conſiſted of a captain, two mates, ſteward and a dozen ſailors—and ſhe alſo had a guard of twelve invalid marines, and about thirty ſoldiers drafted from the Britiſh and Heſſian troops on Long Iſland. The large number confined in the *Jerſey*, ſometimes more than a thouſand at a time, and the terrible ſufferings which they there endured, have made

her name pre-eminent, and her hiftory a fynonym for prifon
fhips during the war.

(24.) Fort Columbus, the U. S. fortification fituated on
Governor's Ifland, in the harbor of New York. This ifland
was originally called, by the Indians, *Pagganck*, and by the
Dutch, *Nutten*, or *Nut Ifland*, from the many nut-bearing trees
formerly growing upon it. Its evident importance as a point
of defence for the harbor, caufed it to be referved by the early
Colonial affembly, " as a fort of demefne for the Govern-
or," with the intention of erecting a fort upon it—but no
fuch ufe was made of it, until after its ceffion to the United
States, by act of the Legiflature, paffed February 15, 1800.

(25.) Henry Morgan, was a grocer, at 30 Peck Slip,
refidence 151 Cherry ftreet.

(26.) Andrew Hegeman, attorney at law, 302 Pearl
ftreet, and refidence 6 Cherry ftreet.

(27.) John Minuse, grocer, at 238 William ftreet, in 1809.

(28.) Ignatius Redmond, accountant, 80 Fair ftreet, in
1809.

(29.) John Walker, cooper, at 82 Liberty ftreet, in
1809.

(30.) PETER IRVING, an elder brother of the more celebrated Washington Irving, graduated at Columbia College, and became a physician. The Directory of 1796 notes him as an M. D., at No. 3 Wall street, and as Surgeon's Mate of the New York Regiment of Artillery, a "crack" organization, commanded by Lieut.-Col. Sebastian Bauman. Of this regiment, which seems to have comprised most of the rising young men of the day, Peter Curtenius was first and De Witt Clinton was second Major. In the year 1802, the *Morning Chronicle* was established as a daily paper, of which he became the editor, and which was discontinued in the autumn of 1805. A year's absence in Europe was followed, on his return, by his entering upon the famous History of New York, in conjunction with his brother Washington— but a sudden call to England on business threw the whole labor of that work upon the latter. In 1810, he became the resident partner in England of the firm of P. & E. Irving, but the firm failed about 1818, and thenceforth he became more identified with his brother's literary labors and travels. In 1820, he published anonymously a Venetian tale, from the French, entitled Giovanni Sbogarro, which was published at New York, and at Birmingham. In 1836, he returned to New York, and died June 27th, 1838. His remains repose in the family vault at Sleepy Hollow, befide thofe of his devotedly-attached brother, Wafhington Irving.

(31.) THE GENERAL SOCIETY OF MECHANICS AND TRADES-MEN, according to tradition, was organized previous to the Revolution, and was, to fome extent, broken up by the ftirring events of that period. Its objects feem to have been the development of a "mutual benefit" among the different trades, the relief of the orphan and the widow, and the affording of means of intellectual attainments to a large clafs of the youth engaged in mechanical employments. Its firft record of organization is dated Nov. 17th, 1785, at the houfe of Walter Heyer, in Pearl, near Cedar ftreet, Robert Boyd, Chairman. From this time to 1792, it feems to have been merely a fort of General Congrefs to which all the trades-focieties in the country fent delegates, and hence arofe its defignation—"General" Society of Mechanics and Tradef-men. It was finally incorporated March 4, 1792. In 1811, this act having expired by its own limitation, another was paffed by which the powers and privileges of the Society were confiderably increafed. In 1821, an amendment was made to this act, whereby the Society was empowered to appropriate fuch part of its funds as may feem expedient "to

the eſtabliſhment and maintenance of a ſchool for the educa-
tion of children of its indigent or deceaſed members," and
alſo, for the eſtabliſhment of an "Apprentices' Library, for
the uſe of the apprentices of the mechanics of New York."
In 1842, this act was renewed and extended to the year
1860, and the Society was authorized to receive pay for
tuition from pupils other than thoſe entitled to gratuitous
inſtruction. From 1783 to 1830, the operations of the Society were chiefly confined to benevolent objects, the relief
of its diſtreſſed members, etc. The Library was eſtabliſhed
at about the ſame time as the ſchool. The Society firſt occupied the old Free School building, corner of Chatham ſtreet
and Tryon row, then a new building on Chambers ſtreet;
afterwards they purchaſed the High School building in
Croſby ſtreet, and, in 1845, removed to their preſent property on Broadway. The Library now numbers 18,000
volumes, the ſchool is one of the beſt and the moſt flouriſh-
ing in the city, and the Society owns conſiderable productive
property. It may alſo claim the honor of having at one
time *refuſed admiſſion to Robert Fulton*, on the ground that
their rules forbade the admiſſion of any to their memberſhip
who were not *practical* mechanics!

(32.) CORNELIUS CRYGIER, a paper hanging manufacturer, at 83 Water ftreet, lived at 18 Warren ftreet. In 1798 was fecond Vice-Prefident of the " General Society of Mechanics and Tradefmen" in New York City.

(33.) ANTHONY STEENBACK, was a builder, at 334 Broadway, a member of the " General Society of Mechanics and Tradefmen."

(34.) JAMES WEBBER LENT, was a prominent merchant, whofe father, John, a matter-builder, had been a captain in Braddock's Expedition, and was prefent when Wolfe fell at Quebec. He was a fierce old fellow, full of fight and frolic; married Ann, daughter of Adrian Hoogland, of New York City, and died in North Carolina in 1768. Two of his children went into bufinefs in New York—*James Webber* and *John*. John was a gold and filver fmith, at No. 18 Naffau ftreet, after the Peace. *James W.* fought all through the Revolutionary War, and at its clofe, married, in 1784, a daughter of Nathan Macomb, and in 1790 opened a grocery on the corner of Little Water and Broad ftreets. In 1798, he had moved into South ftreet, where he kept a flour flore in addition to groceries. In 1802, he received the appoint-

ment of Inſpector of pot and pearl aſhes, and was at No. 92
Broad ſtreet, his reſidence being at 97 Stone ſtreet; and in
1809, his ſtore was 27 Front, and his houſe at 17 South
ſtreet. This office he held for ſeveral years, and alſo that of
Regiſtrar. He died in 1839, leaving a ſon, George W. Lent,
now living.

(35.) Thomas R. Mercein, hard bread maker, at 93
Gold ſtreet, a member of the Legiſlature, from New York
City, in 1811 and 1812, and a very active and public-ſpirited
citizen. He died October 24, 1843.

(36.) John I. Labagh, a ſtone-cutter, at 2 Greenwich
ſtreet, reſided at 15 Thames ſtreet.

(37.) James Hopson, reſided at 24 Vandewater ſtreet, in
1809.

(38.) Gurdon S. Mumford, a merchant of New York,
and for ſix years a member of Congreſs. In 1817, he was
one of the 28 members of the "Brokers of the New-York
Exchange Board."

(39.) Crane Wharf, probably ſo called from old Matthias Crane, a prominent New York merchant of the early

part of the prefent century, was located on the Eaſt River, a little above the foot of Beekman St.

(40.) Ald. Abraham King, grocer, reſided at 61 Dey ſtreet, was Alderman of the 9th Ward in 1804 and 1805, and of the 3d Ward in 1807.

(41.) Ald. Abraham Bloodgood, a ſhipwright, at 100 Harman ſtreet, and a leading man in Tammany; Aſſiſtant Alderman of the 4th Ward in 1804, 1807.

(42.) John D. Miller, was Aſſiſtant Alderman of the 6th Ward in 1805, and Alderman of the ſame Ward in 1806, 1807. A merchant in Broadway near Chambers ſtreet.

(43.) John Pintard, born in New York, May 18, 1759, was a defcendant of a worthy Huguenot emigrè, Anthony Pintard, who ſettled at Shrewſbury, Monmouth Co., N. J. John Pintard, the grandfather of our fubject, was Alderman and Aſſiſtant of the Dock Ward of New York City, from 1738 to 1747; and his father, John Pintard, was a merchant, and married, in 1757, the lovely daughter of John Cannon, a prominent merchant of that day. While on a voyage to the Weſt Indies, as ſupercargo of his own veſſel,

26

in the year 1760, he died at Port-au-Prince; and, his wife having died the year before (three weeks after the birth of her son), young John was left an orphan, and adopted by his uncle, Louis Pintard. As soon as he was old enough, he was sent to the then famous Grammar-school, kept by the Rev. Leonard Cutting, at Hempstead, L. I. Here he remained three years, and attained the reputation of being the best Latin scholar in the school. Going from thence to Princeton College, he was nearly ready to graduate when the Revolutionary War commenced, and partaking of the general enthusiasm which converted the whole college into a camp, he became for awhile a drill-master, and finally, much against the wishes of his friends and instructors, performed a short tour of duty in New York with an artillery company which had been organized under his professor of mathematics. Returning again to college, he received his diploma, and then resided for awhile with his uncle Louis, at his country seat at New Rochelle, and afterwards at Norwalk, Conn. Before long, however, he was made deputy to his uncle, who had been appointed by Gen. Washington, as commissary for the American prisoners incarcerated by the British, in the prisons and prison ships of New York. The arduous and difficult duties of this responsible office were

almoft entirely performed by young Pintard, for a number of
years, to the perfect fatisfaction of all concerned. Releafed
at length, in 1780, from witneffing thefe fcenes of mifery and
outrage, which all his official and perfonal offices could but
flightly affuage or mitigate, he went to Paramus, N. J., the
refidence of a diftant connection, and a noted patriot, Col.
Abraham Brafher. Here he became acquainted with the
Colonel's daughter Eliza, whom, in 1785, he married.
Meantime, in 1782, he had again become a clerk in the
counting-houfe of his uncle Louis, who was one of the firft
and largeft merchants in the Eaft India trade. After his
marriage, however, he commenced bufinefs for himfelf, at
No. 12 Wall ftreet, went into the Eaft India trade, and
bought or built the fhip "Belgiofa," and alfo owned the
"Jay," which was one of the firft veffels that brought
cargoes from China to this port. From 1789 to 1792, he
was, by fucceffive re-elections, affiftant alderman of the Eaft
Ward; and, in 1790, was elected to the Legiflature. In
1792, however, Pintard, then at the height of his fame and
pofition as a fuccefsful merchant, was totally ruined by the
failure of his friend William Duer, whofe notes he had en-
dorfed for over a million of dollars. All his poffeffions—
fhips, houfes, cargoes, furniture, library, etc.—were fold to

satisfy this great debt, but it was not a drop in the bucket. Then, under the cloud of this terrible misfortune, he re- moved to Newark; but there even he was followed by the remorseless creditors of Duer, for whose debts he was finally imprisoned fourteen months in the Newark jail. While there he studied law deeply, with a view to its practice; but, after passing his examination for admission to the Bar, found that he was not calculated for a public speaker, and relin- quished the project. In 1797, he took the benefit of the bankrupt act in New Jersey, and in 1800 availed himself of the general bankrupt law of the United States. After this he resumed business in New York city, as a book-auctioneer, and at this time lived at No. 31 Dey street; he seems, also, to have tried brokerage for a year or so, with but indifferent success. Then he received, from his uncle Louis, a quarter interest in *The Daily Advertiser*, but, for some reason un- known, did not long wield the editorial pen. In 1802, Mr. Pintard went to New Orleans, but did not remain long, and returning was appointed, in the winter of 1804–5, City In- spector and Clerk to the Corporation of New York; his office, at this time, being in the old City Hall, at the corner of Nassau and Wall streets, and his residence at Upper Reade street, No. 11. While occupying this office of City Inspector, he eſtabliſhed, in ſpite of manifold difficulties, the department for the regiſtry of births and deaths in the city; and, as clerk, he was the beſt friend of the firemen, all of the laws moſt conducive to their advantage having been drafted and recommended by him. Theſe two offices which he held were reſigned in 1809, and he was ſucceeded by Gen. Jacob Morton. The ſame year he became ſecretary of the Mutual Inſurance Company, eſtabliſhed in 1787, chartered in 1798, and re-chartered in 1800. Of this old and diſtinguiſhed corporation (better known, ſince 1846, as the "Knickerbocker Fire Inſurance Company") he remained ſecretary for a term of twenty years, and continued to be a director until his deceaſe. In 1828, he was elected Preſident of the New York Savings Bank, an inſtitution which he had founded, in connection with De Witt Clinton and others, in 1816, and this office he continued to hold until his deceaſe in 1844, aged 86 years.

It has well been ſaid of him, that "there never lived that man in the city, who could ſtart great meaſures, as John Pintard could do. He could indite a hand-bill that would inflame the minds of the people for any good work. He could call a meeting with the pen of a poet, and before the people met, he would have arranged the doings for a per-feet fuccefs.   He knew the weak point of every man, and he would gratify the vanity of men, and get their money, without any of them fufpecting that they were merely the refpectable names and moneyed tools that Mr. Pintard required." In 1787, he was mainly inftrumental in procuring from the Legiflature, a charter for the Bank of New York ; and was, alfo, the one who caufed the old names of fome of the ftreets of New York—fuch as King, Queen, Duke, Princefs, &c.— to be changed to good republican names.   In 1791, as one of the Tammany Society, he was the originator, and afterwards the fecretary, of the American Mufeum, founded by that Order,—afterwards Baker's, then Scudder's, and *now* Barnum's American Mufeum.   Of the Tammany Society, as we have before faid, he was a founder and a brother in high ftanding —for fome years a Grand Sachem—and in the proceffion with which that Order celebrated their anniverfary in May, 1791, Pintard was a prominent object.   He was dreffed in the full Tammany coftume, but there was not an article upon his perfon that was not of American manufacture.   The buttons of his coat were of American conk-fhell, fet in rims of American filver.   He was the "enlightened founder," as one of his compeers ftyles him, of the New York Hiftorical Society, in 1804, and its firft librarian ; alfo a truftee of the New York Society

Library, founded in 1772, and afterwards among the origina-
tors of the Merchants' and the Mercantile Libraries. On
the 19th of February, 1805, he was one of the twelve perfons who laid the foundations of the admirable " Free-School
Syftem" of the city. In 1807, he took a very active part in
the procuring of the Act which appointed a Commiffion of
Streets and Roads in the City of New York, under whofe
action the prefent fplendid fyftem of ftreets and avenues was
commenced. He was alfo one of the incorporators of the
Chamber of Commerce, and when, after the Revolutionary
War, it was dormant, he re-vitalized it, and was its fecretary from 1807 to 1827. Of the American Bible Society,
eftablifhed in 1816, he was one of the founders, and a prominent member, being at one time its fecretary, and afterwards a Vice-Prefident. To the Brooklyn Steamboat Company, he was, for many years, fecretary; and when the
Mechanics' Bank of New York was chartered in 1810, he
was ftrongly preffed to become cafhier, but declined. In
1812, he was appointed by the Common Council of the
City to fign all the paper notes of a fmall denomination,
iffued by that body, at that time, as well as during the war.
The Savings Bank, eftablifhed in 1816, was engineered by
Pintard, who, after he had feen it fairly under way in 1819,

withdrew from all connection with it, but, in 1828, was elected its Prefident, and continued to hold that office until 1842. He it was, alfo, who made the tranflation of the Englifh Common Prayer-Book into French, the verfion now ufed in the French Epifcopal Church of this city. The great Erie Canal owes its very exiftence to the ftrenuous and perfiftent efforts, through a long feries of years, of John Pintard—he planned the arrangements for the magnificent celebration of its completion, and carried, on that occafion, the bottle of Lake Erie water that was emptied into the At-lantic, as an emblem of the union of the outfide and inland feas. The Houfe of Refuge and the Sailors' Retreat were among his pets—and the Theological Seminary of the Epif-copal Church owes much to him—for he collected, with infinite tact, thoufands of dollars (probably over $100,000) for that inftitution. Lengthy as this fketch is, it affords but a curfory view of the life-long labors and beneficent deeds of John Pintard, whom profperity did not fpoil, and whofe ufefulnefs adverfity could not leffen.

(44.) JOEL HART, M. D., was, in 1808, at 29 Water ftreet, and in 1809, at 16 Dey ftreet.

(45.) DE WITT CLINTON, the fon of a General of the

Revolution, was born March 2, 1769, at Little Britain, Orange County, N. Y. He graduated at Columbia College, in 1786, became a lawyer, and, shortly after, private secretary to his uncle, George Clinton, the first Republican Governor of New York. He was appointed, in time, secretary to the Board of Regents of the University, and also to the Board of Fortifications of New York. In 1797, he was elected to the Legislature, and in 1801, was chosen to the United States Senate, of which body he remained a member two sessions. He was then annually elected Mayor of the City of New York, from 1803 to 1815, except in 1807 and 1810. In 1812, he was an unsuccessful candidate for the Presidency of the United States. In 1817, he was elected, almost unanimously, Governor of the State of New York, by a union of the two great parties for that purpose. In 1820, he was re-elected, in spite of the adherents of Daniel D. Tompkins, then Vice-President of the United States. He declined to become a candidate in 1822, but his removal from the office of Canal Commissioner, which happened in 1823, roused such a feeling in regard to him, that, in 1824, he was again triumphantly re-elected to the Governorship. In 1826, he was once more elected Governor, but died before the expiration of his term, on the 11th of February, 1828.

27

Always alive to every good work, he is remembered as one of the founders of the New York Hiſtorical Society, the Academy of Arts, and the Orphan Aſylum, as well as many other important public enterpriſes. But his moſt enduring monument is the great Erie Canal, which owes its exiſtence to his intereſt, influence and perſeverance.

(46.) CLARKSON CROLIUS, was born in the 6th Ward, in New York City, on the ſame ſpot where his grandfather, the firſt ſtoneware manufacturer in the city had ſettled. In 1802, the Republican party elected him Aſſiſtant Alderman of his Ward, a poſt which he held, by re-election, until 1805, when his party choſe him as a Repreſentative to the State Legiſlature. Here alſo, he continued, by ſucceſſive re-elections, until 1825, when, by unanimous vote of the Houſe, he was made Speaker. For many years Grand Sachem of the Tammany Society, he laid, in 1811, the corner-ſtone of Tammany Hall. In 1812, he was commiſſioned as colonel by Preſident Madiſon, and ſerved on duty at the Narrows until the cloſe of the War. After 1827, Mr. Crolius mingled no more in public life, and died in the houſe of his birth, in 1843, aged ſeventy-one years.

(47.) Captain JAMES HEWETT, author of the Wallabout Grand March, kept a mufical repofitory, at 59 Maiden lane.

(48.) The frigate CONSTITUTION, was one of fix veffels conftructed by law of Congrefs, dated March 27th, 1794. She was built at Bofton, was rated as a 44-gun fhip, and was launched on the 20th of September, 1797. She ftarted on her firft cruife July 20, 1798, under Captain Samuel Nicholfon, on the coaft fouthward of Cape Henry. In the beginning of 1800 we find the Conftitution flying the broad pennant of Commodore Talbot, on the St. Domingo ftation, and that year, a floop, manned by her officers and crew, performed the brilliant exploit of cutting out a French *letter of marque* from Porte Platte. In 1803, the Conftitution, bearing the broad pennant of Commodore Preble, formed one of the fquadron engaged in the war againft Tripoli, where fhe took a confpicuous part in the attacks and bombardment of that town. In the latter part of this year Commodore Preble returned home, and Captain Decatur took command of the Conftitution, which, in November following, paffed under the command of Captain John Rodgers, fenior officer of the fleet. In the beginning of the War of 1812, the Conftitution, then commanded by Captain Hull, was fent to Europe, having on board fpecie for the payment of the intereſt on the debt due to Holland. After her return, having ſhipped a new crew, ſhe ſailed on a cruiſe northward from Annapolis; and on the 17th of July was ſurrounded by and eſcaped from a fleet of Britiſh veſſels, by a chaſe which has become hiſtorical in the American navy, from its length, cloſeneſs and activity. On the 19th of Auguſt, while engaged in doing conſiderable damage to the enemy's ſhipping, near the Iſle of Sables, the Conſtitution fell in with the Britiſh ſhip-of-war *Guerriere*, which, after a brief but deſperate action, ſurrendered to the American captain.

Captain Hull, having ſhortly after reſigned the command of his ſhip, was ſucceeded by Commodore Bainbridge, who, on the 29th of December, brought her into action with the Britiſh frigate *Java*, 38 guns, which alſo ſurrendered to her, after a ſevere two hours' fight. The Conſtitution ſoon came under the command of Commodore Stewart; and, in 1813, underwent repairs, taking the ſea again in the winter of 1814, when ſhe made a cruiſe to the ſouthward, capturing the Britiſh war ſchooner *Pictou*, 14, beſides ſome other prizes. On the 20th of February, 1815, ſhe met and conquered the *Cyane*, 24, and the *Levant*, 18 guns, in fair fight. "Thus terminated," ſays Cooper, "the exploits of the gallant Conſtitution, or Old Ironſides, as ſhe was affectionately called in the navy. * *   In the courſe of two years and nine months, this ſhip had been in three actions, had been twice critically chaſed, and had captured five veſſels of war, two of which were frigates, and a third frigate-built.   In all her ſervice, as well before Tripoli as in this war, her good fortune was remarkable.   She never was diſmaſted, never got aſhore, nor ſcarcely ever ſuffered any of the uſual accidents of the ſea.   Though ſo often in battle, no very ſerious ſlaughter ever took place on board her. * *   Her entire career had been that of what is uſually called a ‘ lucky ſhip.’ Her fortune, however, may perhaps be explained in the ſimple fact that ſhe had always been well commanded.   In her two laſt cruiſes ſhe had probably poſſeſſed as fine a crew as ever manned a frigate.   They were principally New England men, and it has been ſaid of them, that they were almoſt qualified to fight the ſhip without her officers."

The Conſtitution was the flag-ſhip of the Mediterranean ſquadron, under Commodore J. D. Elliott, in 1837; under Commodore D. Turner in the Pacific ſquadron in 1841; and again, in 1846, under Captain F. A. Percival.   In 1855, was Commodore Mayo's flag-ſhip on the coaſt of Africa, and in 1861 was at the Naval School in Annapolis, Md., where, refcued by the gallantry of the cadets from being feized by the rebels, fhe was fent to Newport, R. I., whither the School was alfo transferred, and where fhe now ferves the purpofe of a fchool-fhip.

(49.) Commodore JOHN RODGERS, born in Maryland, in 1771, entered the U. S. Navy as a lieutenant, March 9, 1798, and was the executive officer (com. Capt. March 5, 1799) of the frigate Conftellation, the flag-fhip of Commodore Truxton, when fhe captured the French frigate L'Infurgente, Feb. 9, 1799. Was after engaged in the Tripolitan war, in the frigate John Adams, 28, and afterwards in the frigate Congrefs, 38, performing feveral gallant exploits, and in 1805 fucceeded Commodore Barron in the command of that fquadron. In the fpring of 1811, while in command of the Prefident, 44, he overhauled, and after a brief fight, captured the Britifh fhip Little Belt, 22 guns, which had impreffed a feaman from an American brig off Sandy Hook. On June 21, 1812, within an hour after receiving official intelligence of the declaration of war by the United States, againft Great Britain, he failed from New York, in the Prefident, in command of a fquadron ; and on June 23d fell in with, chafed and engaged, with his own fhip, the Britifh fhip Belvidera, 36,

which eventually efcaped. During this cruife, which occupied about 70 days, he captured 7 Britifh merchantmen,
and re-captured one American veffel. Several other cruifes
were made by him during the war, and feveral cap-
tures made. In June 1814, he was appointed to the command of the new frigate Guerriere, and rendered important
fervices in the defence of Baltimore. From April 1815, to
Dec. 1824, he ferved as Prefident of the Board of Navy
Commiffioners, and from 1824 to 1827, in command of the
Mediterranean fquadron. On his return, he was again appointed to the Board of Navy Commiffioners, which he re-
linquifhed in 1837, on account of declining health. At his
death, which occurred at Philadelphia, in Auguft 1838, he was
the fenior officer of the American Navy.

(50.) JOHN FLEMING, of 65 North Moore ftreet, in 1809.

(51.) GEORGE W. BROWN, a dry goods dealer, at 127
Chatham ftreet, in 1809.

(52.) DANIEL DODGE, was in the millinery bufinefs, in
1809, and was alfo city-meafurer, at 374 Pearl ftreet.

(53.) JOSEPH WORRELL, laborer, in 1809, at 31 Bedlow
ftreet, and an active Tammany-ite.

(54.) Now FULTON FERRY, at the foot of Fulton ftreet, Brooklyn.

(55.) Now FULTON STREET, Brooklyn.

(56.) BENJAMIN AYCRIGG, was born in New Jerfey, Sept. 27, 1773. His father, John Hurft Aycrigg, was one of feven fons, born at Upton-on-the-Severn, England, ftudied furgery with Dr. Kater, of London ; was the only member of the family that left England; went to Granada, then to New York before our Revolution, fettled as a phyfician at the "Englifh Neighborhood," N. J., and married the fifter of Dominie Lydecker, who was a graduate of King's (now Co-lumbia) College, New York, and of Holland defcent. On the 6th of June, 1795, Benjamin Aycrigg married Sufan Bancker, daughter of John Bancker, whofe property in the city of New York was burned during the great fire, while he was in the Revolutionary fervice. He ferved five years in the army; was a captain, and engaged in the expedition to Canada. His brother, Gerard Bancker, was for twenty years Treafurer of the State of New York. They were de-fcended from Garret Bancker and Elizabeth Dirks, both born in Holland, and married in New Amfterdam, April 10, 1658. The mother of Sufan Bancker was the daughter of Francis

Mefnard, whofe Huguenot anceftor was brought over to this country by his guardian, Governor Dubois, in his flight from France, on the Revocation of the Edict of Nantes, in 1685. Her uncle, ——— Mefnard, was captain of a veffel failing between New York and St. Thomas, W. I. He was confined, for fome time, in the " Provoft," New York, and was called, by Cunningham the jailor, "a damned rebel that ought to be hung," when fome of his female relatives ventured to vifit him during his confinement. He was fortunately releafed, juft in time to prevent him from being ftarved to death by the inhumanity of his jailors.

Benjamin Aycrigg, was a merchant, and a major in the N. Y. artillery. He belonged to the Wafhington Chapter of Royal Arch Mafons; the keyftone and Bible of that Chapter are yet in the poffeffion of his family. He never held a political office, but was an active Democrat at the time that a protective tariff was a favorite principle with "Old Tammany," and we have it on good authority, that, as a Tammany delegate, he nominated " Daniel D. Tompkins, the farmer's fon," when he was elected Governor of the State of New York. In 1808, he was Sachem of the Pennfylvania, or Rattlefnake tribe of Tammany; and his place of bufinefs was in the Greenwich Market. In 1815

28

he lived in Greenwich ftreet, in one of the four houfes ftill ftanding, oppofite Vandam ftreet, where he had the Ex-King Jofeph Buonaparte as a next door neighbor. Mr. Aycrigg died April 22, 1817, having been, for the latter portion of his life, fomewhat retired from active bufinefs. His fon, Colonel Benjamin Aycrigg, of Paffaic, N. J., is a moft worthy defcendant of fo excellent a man ; and his intereft and labors in behalf of the Sanitary Commiffion, during the prefent war, entitle him to more than a mere paffing notice.

(57.) The ground around the prefent Navy-Yard, was, at the time of thefe ceremonies, quite high ; and there were feveral hills or eminences in the neighborhood, fuch as " Vinegar Hill," and " McKenzie's One Tree Hill," any one of which would have formed advantageous pofitions both for the artillery and the fpectators.

(58.) BENJAMIN ROMAINE (or, as the name fhould be more properly fpelled, *Romeyn*), was of French extraction, and a native of the city of New York. At the commencement of the Revolutionary War, he was a mere lad at fchool, preparing for admiffion to King's (now Columbia) College, but upon the occupation of the city by the Britifh army, his father's family retired to the neighborhood of Hackenfack, in New Jerfey. His ftudies being thus interrupted by "war's rude alarms," he enlifted in the American army, and ferved feveral terms of fix months each, finally attaining the rank of fergeant, and was engaged in feveral hotly-contefted fkirmifhes. He was, finally, taken prifoner, and immerfed in two of the prifons in New York, from which, after a confinement of feven weeks, he was releafed, by exchange, in October, 1781. After the clofe of the war, his family having fuffered confiderably in the lofs of their property, young Romaine opened a fchool, for both fexes, at 37 Partition ftreet (now 198 Fulton), New York, where he foon eftablifhed a very good reputation as a teacher—numbering among his pupils, Wafhington Irving, Profeffor John Anthon, the late Judge J. T. Irving, and others fince diftinguifhed in the literary, profeffional, and focial circles of the city.

In the fpring of 1797, being then about 30 years of age, the condition of his health obliged him to relinquifh teaching; and, as he had, by his economical habits and natural thrift, accumulated a competency fufficiently ample for his wants, he never afterward engaged in any regular bufinefs. For many years he refided in Hudfon ftreet, New York, and in 1808, lived at No. 97 Church ftreet.

In politics, he was a Democrat, and in 1808, was Grand Sachem of Tammany Society. He alſo held the office of Comptroller during the mayoralty of De Witt Clinton, to whom he formed an antipathy which made him a violent "bucktail," as the members of the anti-Clinton wing of "Old Tammany" were called. In the War of 1812, he was a ſtrong Jefferſonian, and ſuſtained the vigorous proſecution of the war, during which he held an important departmental poſition, with the rank of major.

During the latter portion of his life, Mr. Romaine employed himſelf in the care of his extenſive property in ſeveral parts of the city, and in literary purſuits. His reading was chiefly confined to hiſtory, politics, and the ſcience of government, and his pen was conſtantly employed in contributing to the preſs, (under the *nom de plume* of " An Old Citizen,") articles upon the paſſing and important topics of the day. In 1832, he publiſhed a pamphlet,* in which he vigorouſly aſſailed the doctrine of State Rights as then advocated by the Nullifiers of South Carolina, and with a pre-

---

* STATE SOVEREIGNTY, *and a Certain Diſſolution of the Union. By Benjamin Romaine, An Old Citizen of New-York. To the Hon. John C. Calhoun, now Vice-Preſident of the United States. New-York : J. Kennaday, Printer, No. 2 Dey ſtreet.* 1832. *8vo.,* 54 *pages.*

science which, in the light of recent events, feems moft remarkable, fortells the confequences of fuch principles.

In literary, as well as perfonal character, Mr. Romaine
may be faid to have been diftinguifhed, not fo much for any
efpecial range, or brilliancy of intellect, as for foundnefs of
underftanding, elevated views, and high moral integrity.
Although Mr. Romaine was not a profeffing Chriftian, but
rather a moralift ; and, although "Pope's Effay on Man,"
(which he knew by heart) was probably a greater favorite
with him than the Bible—yet he refpected and valued the
ordinances of Chriftianity—and, in his own life, was a
bright examplar of all its virtues. In his perfonal habits, he
was remarkably cleanly and orderly ; liquor and tobacco, in
any form, were very obnoxious to him, and his manner of
life was extremely fimple, frugal and temperate. Poffeffing
great pride of character, with very little vanity, he paffed
through life unoftentatioufly, but with comfort to himfelf,
and with the refpect of others. His perfonal appearance
has been defcribed as tall, flim, and commanding in figure;
with great vigor of body and motion, and with a countenance difplaying ferioufnefs mingled with kindnefs and affa-
bility.

Indeed, this kindnefs of heart was always manifefted, except when he came in contact with Englifhmen. Then his prejudices quickly and unmiftakably manifefled themfelves, and amufing ftories are yet related of the rough manner in which he would abfolutely refufe to treat with any Englifh-man who applied to become a tenant of any of his houfes. Indeed, the recollection of what he had fuffered, and of the horrors which he had witneffed in the Britifh prifons, filled his mind with intenfe hatred of Britifh rule, and of anything pertaining to it, which he could never banifh from his mind.

It was this, alfo, in great meafure, which influenced him, in 1839, when the lot in Brooklyn, on which the bones of the Martyrs of the Prifon Ships had been buried, were *fold for Taxes*, to become its purchafer; and it was this which, through all his fubfequent life, made him cling with jealous care to the cuftody of thefe remains—conftantly protefting againft any difpofal being made of them, *except* by the *General Government*, which he rightly confidered as the *only proper cuftodian*.

It has been a fincere pleafure thus to collect all the information concerning this honeft, patriotic and ufeful citizen; and we can only regret, that the moft diligent inquiries which we have made, have refulted in eliciting fo little information concerning him.

(59.) NASSAU ISLAND, the name given to Long Ifland, by the Colonial Governor, Benj. Fletcher, by an act dated April 10, 1693. This alteration, which was a mere freak of political vanity, was neither popular or generally adopted; and the act, although, it is believed, never explicitly repealed, was fuffered to become obfolete by difufe.

(60.) JOSEPH D. FAY, attorney and counfellor at law, 26 White ftreet.

(61.) Col. ISAAC HAYNE, one of the earlieft patriots of South Carolina who took the field, and, at the fiege of Charlefton, in 1780, had command of a company of mounted militia, being at the time a member of the State Legiflature. Having, from motives of family affection, been forced to take the oath of allegiance to the King, he remained neutral in act (though not in his feelings) until in 1781, the condition of affairs had fo changed, that he felt releafed from its obligations; and again took up arms for his country, as commander of a cavalry troop. He was, however, captured in battle, and hung by the Britifh Colonel Balfour, as a traitor to Great Britain. His death, and its attending circumftances, excited the greateft attention and commifferation, both in Europe and America, it being confidered as marking the character of the British commandant with the foul ftain of difhonor and favage cruelty. He died July 31, 1781 —and thirty-two years afterwards, Lord Rawdon, one of the principals in the affair, attempted to excufe his want of humanity, in a letter to Gen. Henry Lee, (fee his *Memoirs*, page 459,) by pleading the juftice of the fentence. But the denunciations of the Duke of Richmond, in the Houfe of Lords, at the time, and the facts of hiftory, have irrevocably ftamped the whole tranfaction with the ftamp of barbarifm.

(62.) Capt. WILLIAM CUNNINGHAM, an Irifhman by birth, and a brute by nature, who, during the occupation of New York by the Britifh, occupied the poft of Provoft-Marfhal of the city. The following autobiographical confeffion, which firft appeared in one of the Englifh papers, about 1794, and which has always been held as authentic, affords all that we know concerning him.

*The Life, Confeffion, and laft dying Words of Capt. Cunningham, formerly Britifh Provoft-Marfhal in the City of New-York, who was executed in London, the 10th of Auguft, 1791.**

* Although the dates, hiftorical and local allufions of this confeffion, are correct, and fubftantiated by contemporaneous data—yet its genuinenefs can only be fatisfactorily determined by reference to the London newfpapers, or

I, WILLIAM CUNNINGHAM, was born in Dublin Barracks, in the year 1738. My father was trumpeter in the Blue Dragoons; and at the age of eight years, I was placed with an officer as his fervant, in which ftation I continued until I was fixteen, and being a great proficient in horfemanfhip, was taken as an affiftant to the riding-mafter of the troop, and in 1761, was made fergeant of dragoons; but the Peace* coming the year following, I was difbanded. Being bred to no profeffion, I took up with a woman who kept a gin-fhop in a blind alley, near the Cole Quay, but the houfe being fearched for ftolen goods, and my doxy taken to Newgate, I thought it proper to decamp; accordingly I fet off for the North, and arrived at Drogheda, where, in a few months after, I married the daughter of an excifeman, by whom I had three fons. About the year 1772, we removed to Newry, where I commenced the profeffion of fcaw-banker, which is that of enticing mechanics and country people to fhip themfelves for America, on promife of great advantage,

Newgate records. It firft appeared on this fide of the water, in a Philadel-phia paper, towards the clofe of 1791 (about the time it would probably reach there from England), and is mentioned as juft received from London, and as *authentic*. (*Onderdonk.*)

* The Spanifh war commenced 1762, and ended the fame or next year. (*Onderdonk.*)

29

and then artfully getting an indenture upon them, in confequence of which, on their arrival in America, they were fold,
or obliged to ferve a term of years for their paffage.   I embarked at Newry, in the ſhip Needham, for New-York, and
arrived at that port the 4th day of Auguſt, 1774,* with ſome
indented ſervants I had kidnapped in Ireland; but they were
liberated in New-York, on account of the bad uſage they
had received from me during the paffage.   In that city I uſed
the profeſſion of breaking horſes, and teaching ladies and
gentlemen to ride; but rendering myſelf obnoxious† to the
citizens in their infant ſtruggle for freedom, I was obliged to
fly on board the Aſia man-of-war, and from thence to Boſton,
where my own oppoſition to the meaſures purſued by the
Americans in ſupport of their rights, was the firſt thing that
recommended me to the notice of Gen. Gage; and when the

* Yeſterday arrived the Needham, Capt. Cheevers, with 300 paffengers
from Newry.   The times of ſervants of both ſexes to be diſpoſed of, (to pay
for their paffage.)   *Rivington's Gazette, Aug.* 4, 1774.

† In 1775, Cunningham and a companion got among ſome " Liberty
Boys," who ſeized and dragged them to the Liberty-pole, and endeavored
to make them kneel and " d——n the popiſh King George"—from which
indignity, however, he was reſcued by the police.   (*See Rivington's Gazette,*
March 9, 1775.)

war commenced, I was oppointed Provoſt-Marſhall* to the Royal army, which placed me in a ſituation to wreak my vengeance on the Americans. *I ſhudder to think of the murders I have been acceſſory to, both with and without orders from Government, eſpecially while in New-York*, during which time there *were more than* 2000 *priſoners ſtarved in the different churches, by ſtopping their rations, which I ſold.*† *There were alſo* 275 *American priſoners and obnoxious perſons executed, out of all which number there were only about one dozen public executioos, which chiefly conſiſted of Britiſh and Heſſian deſerters. The mode for private executions was thus conducted: a guard was diſpatched from the Provoſt, about half-paſt twelve at night, to the Barrack ſtreet, and the neighborhood of the upper barracks, to order the people to ſhut their window ſhutters, and put out their lights, forbidding them at*

---

* One William Jones had been Gen. Gage's Provoſt-Marſhal till 1775, after which his name no longer appears. (*Onderdonk.*)

† Common fame charged Cunningham with ſelling, and even poiſoning the priſoners' food, exchanging good for bad proviſions, and continuing to draw their rations after their death, or, as they worded it : " he fed the dead, and ſtarved the living." It was not till the ſpring of 1783, towards the cloſe of the war, that a monthly liſt of priſoners was printed in Rivington's Gazette. (*Onderdonk.*)

the same time to presume to look out of their windows and doors on pain of death,* after which the unfortunate prisoners were conducted, gagged, just behind the upper barracks, and hung without ceremony, and there buried by the black pioneer of the Provost. At the end of the war, I returned to England with the army, and settled in Wales, as being a cheaper place of living than in any of the populous cities; but being at length persuaded to go to London, I entered so warmly into the dissipations of that capital, that I soon found my circumstances much embarrassed, to relieve which I mortgaged my half-pay to an army agent; but that being soon expended, I forged a draft, of £300 sterling, on the Board of Ordnance, but being detected in presenting it for acceptance, I was apprehended, tried and convicted, and for that offence am here to suffer an ignominious death. I beg the prayers of all good Christians, and also pardon and forgiveness of God for the many horrid murders I have been accessory to.

WILLIAM CUNNINGHAM.

* Watson, in his Annals of New York, states that Cunningham hung five or six of a night, until the women of the neighborhood, distressed by the cries and pleadings of the prisoners for mercy, petitioned Howe to have the practice discontinued.

(63.) This Liberty-pole ſtood at the foot of Fulton ſtreet, Brooklyn, near the old market, which finally came to be regarded as a nuiſance, and was torn down one night, in 1814, by a party of young men. The ſite of the market is now marked by the flag-ſtaff which ſtands in the middle of Fulton ſtreet, near the Ferry-houſe.

(64.) The following notices taken from the public prints of the day, are here inſerted, as properly belonging to the Narrative.—(Editor.)

From the New-York Public Advertiſer.

GRAND FUNERAL PROCESSION,
At the Wallabout, (Long Island.)

The Committee appointed by the Tammany Society, or Columbian Order, of the city of New-York, to make arrangements for the interment of the relics of American ſeamen, ſoldiers, and citizens, who periſhed in the cauſe of liberty and their country, on board the Jerſey and other priſon ſhips of the Britiſh, at the Wallabout, during the Revolution, give notice, that the funeral proceſſion will take place on Wedneſday, the 25th of May inſt.

The particulars of the plan of arrangements will be published as foon before the day on which the proceffion is to take place as poffible.

The Society by which this committee have been appointed are anxious that their fellow-citizens generally fhould participate in the performance of this undertaking, which can be confidered in no other light than that of a national duty, the difcharge of which is calculated to refleft honor on individual exertion, and the country at large.

That the bones of 11,500 of the brave heroes and martyrs of the independence we now enjoy, who were facrificed by the mercilefs cruelty and barbarity of the enemies of that independence, fhould, for five-and-twenty years, have been fuffered to remain uncovered and unprotefted on the foil which gave them birth, is indeed a reproach which can no longer be endured, and muft be done away.

> By order of the Committee,
>
> JACOB VANDERVORT, *Chairman,*
>
> ROBERT TOWNSEND, Junr., *Sec'ry.*

May 6.

NOTICE.—The Wallabout Committee has the fatisfaftion of announcing to their fellow-citizens that the Vault, intended to contain the remains of American prisoners who perished on board the prison ships of the enemy at the Wallabout during the Revolution, is now finished.

By a resolution of the Tammany Society, the grand funeral procession will take place on the 25th inst. In paying this debt of national gratitude, it is hoped that all classes of citizens will participate.

The military commanders, and committees of different societies, military companies and public bodies, in Brooklyn and in this city, are requested to meet at Martling's, This Evening, at seven o'clock, to hear the report of arrangements intended for the occasion.

By order of the Committee,

Jacob Vandervort, *Chairman*,

Robert Townsend, Junr., *Sec'ty*.

May 6, 1808.

From the Aurora, May 28, 1808.

Patriotism.—Eight soldiers of the Revolution arrived here yesterday, from Connecticut, for the purpose of attending the interment of the remains of the martyrs at the Wallabout. They had themselves suffered the loathsome imprisonment, and are among the surviving few who escaped the terrors of the British hulks.—*Pub. Adv.*

IN COMMON COUNCIL.

New-York, May 23, 1808.

The committee appointed to confer with the committee of Tammany Society, begged leave to and recommended the following refolutions, which were agreed to:

Whereas, a refpectful application hath been made to the Common Council by a committee of the Tammany Society, or Columbian Order, inviting the concurrence and co-operation of this Board in the plan of arrangements for inter-ring the remains of the American feamen who perifhed on board the Jerfey prifon fhip at the Wallabout, during the Revolution: And, whereas, the Common Council do con-ceive this undertaking to be highly laudable and patriotic, and that the due execution of it is a public and national duty: And, whereas, the interment is to take place on Wed-nefday, the 25th inft., Therefore,

Refolved, That this Board do recommend that the citizens do obferve the fame day in as refpectful a manner as may be confiftent with their avocations, and that as far as may be convenient they do unite in fetting the fame apart to the commemoration of our brave but unfortunate countrymen who perifhed on board of the Britifh prifon fhips during the Revolutionary War, and for the interment of their remains.

Refolved, That it be recommended, that the different church-bells, and the bells on board the fhips in the harbor, be tolled feventeen minutes, to commence at fun-rife on faid day, and alfo during the proceffion.

Refolved, That it be recommended that the colors of the different veffels in the port be hoifted at half-maft during the faid day.

Refolved, That this Board will attend the proceffion which is to take place on the faid day.

Refolved, That the leffees of the public wharves and flips, and ferry-mafters, be, and they are hereby, requefted to caufe all boats and veffels of every defcription, except ferry-boats, to be removed from the flips at the end of the Fly Market and New Market.

By order of Common Council,

John Pintard, *Clerk.*

(65.) Gen. Jacob Morton, a prominent politician, of the moderate Federal fchool, was elected Alderman in the fall of 1803, and was fubfequently, at feveral times, an unfuccefsful candidate for that office. In January, 1807, he was appointed City Comptroller of New York, and, in 1809, fucceeded Mr. Pintard as Clerk of the Common Council, which place he held for 26 years, and died of apoplexy while yet in office, in December, 1836, aged over 80 years. His family refidence, yet ftanding, was at No. 9 State ftreet, near the Battery. He was a Major-General of N. Y. State Militia.

(66.) Gen. GERARD STEDDIFORD, a commiffion merchant at 77 Wall ftreet, and refiding at No. 2 Robinfon ftreet.

(67.) GARRET SICKLES, boot and fhoe maker, 29 Water ftreet.

(68.) Capt. ALEXANDER COFFIN, whofe narrative is given on pages 43–59.

(69.) An honorary inftitution eftablifhed at the clofe of the Revolution, among the officers of the army and navy, in order to perpetuate the long-cherifhed friendfhip and focial intercourfe which had bound them together during the war. It was, at the fuggeftion of Gen. Knox, and with the approval of Wafhington, formed in May, 1783, and was divided into State Societies. Wafhington was its firft Prefident-General, from 1783 till his death in 1799. He was fucceeded by Gen. Alexander Hamilton, until his death in 1804; his fucceffor was Gen. Charles C. Pinckney of

South Carolina, who died in 1825, fince which the office has been held by Maj.-Gen. Thomas Pinckney, Col. Aaron Ogden, Gen. Morgan Lewis, Maj. Popham, and Gen. Dearborn.

(70.) Rev. JOHN TOWNLY, was a Congregational clergyman in this city. In 1804, he eftablifhed a religious meeting in an old frame building, then ftanding on Warren ftreet, juft out of Broadway. A confiderable number of perfons attended on his miniftry, and a Congregational church was formed. The number of original members cannot now be afcertained, but in the courfe of 3 or 4 years the number of communicants had increafed to nearly 100. Mr. Townly continued to labor in the church for the fpace of 4 or 5 years. The congregation afterwards erected a larger place of worfhip in Elizabeth ftreet, between Walker and Hefter ftreets, where they removed about 1809. Mr. Townly continued in the new church about 4 or 5 years, when he refigned and left the city. The church being much in debt for their new building, became at length fo embarraffed that they were compelled foon after to fell their place of meeting, to the Afbury (colored) Methodifts, whereupon Townly's congregation fcattered. In 1808, he refided at 6 Canal ftreet.

(71.) Rev. RALPH WILLISTON, was preacher in the Zion Church in the city of New York, in 1811. He was instituted Rector in 1813, and continued to officiate as such until the year 1815, when the church building was confumed by fire. This church was built in 1801, by a fociety of Lutherans. It was fituated on Mott ftreet, corner of Crofs. The building was but a fmall one. In 1810, the church was received into communion with the Epifcopal church. Mr. Willifton died in Hempftead, L. I., in the year 1839, aged 65. In 1808, he refided at 33 Mott ftreet.

(72.) There was an order of the Tammany Society, who wore in their hats as an infignia, on certain occafions, a por-tion of the tail of a deer. They were a leading order, and from this circumftance, the friends of Mr. Clinton gave thofe who adopted the views of the members of the Tammany Society in relation to him, the name of *Bucktails;* which name was eventually applied to their friends and fupporters in the country. Hence, the party oppofed to the adminif-tration of Mr. Clinton was, for a long time, called the *Bucktail party.—Hammond.*

(73.) The WISKINKIE was the doorkeeper of the Lodge.

(74.) SAMUEL OSGOOD, was the fon of Capt. Peter

Ofgood, and was born in Andover, N. H., Feb. 14, 1748, and graduated at Harvard College in 1770. On leaving college he commenced the ftudy of theology, with the intention of entering the miniftry, but clofe application fo impaired his health and eyes, that he was compelled to give up the idea, and went into mercantile bufinefs. Soon after the commencement of the Revolution, he was chofen a member of the Provincial Congrefs, and appointed one of the Board of War. He was one of the Convention for planning the State Conftitution, in 1779, and, in 1781, was appointed a Reprefentative in the Continental Congrefs. In the years 1775 and 1776, he was an aid to Gen. Ward. In 1785, when the Treafury of the United States was put under the management of three commiffioners, he was appointed one of them. Each commiffioner was required to give bonds in the penal fum of $100,000. Being unwilling to requeft fo great a favor of his friends, as to afk them to become his fureties to fo large an amount, he hefitated about accepting the office, whereupon the government of Maffachufetts had fuch confidence in him, as to become voluntarily refponfible for him. He continued in office till the eftablifhment of the Conftitution, and the organization of the government, in 1789, when Gen. Wafhington appointed him Poftmafter-

General. He held this office for two years. In 1801, he was Supervifor of New-York, and in 1803, appointed naval officer for the port of New-York, which laft office he held at the time of his death. He was a man of piety, an elder of one of the churches in New-York, and publifhed feveral works, among which was one on Chronology—another " Remarks on Daniel and Revelation," " A Letter on Epifcopacy," &c. He died on the 12th Auguft, 1813, aged 65.

(75.) Col. HENRY RUTGERS, was a patriot of the Revolution, and fought at Brooklyn Heights. His houfe was occupied by the Britifh, during the occupation of New-York, as a hofpital and barracks. In 1797, he prefented to the 1ft Prefbyterian Church in New-York city a lot of ground, lying on the corner of Rutgers and Henry ftreets, for the fite of a church. The church was erected fhortly afterwards. It was a fpacious frame building, meafuring 86 feet by 64, and was called the "Rutgers ftreet Church," and was firft opened for public worfhip May 13, 1798. In 1807, he delivered an addrefs on laying the corner-ftone of the Reformed Dutch Church, in Orchard ftreet.

The old Rutgers Medical Còllege, fince confolidated with

the College of Phyſicians and Surgeons, was named after him, and was largely indebted to his liberality.

Col. Rutgers was a man of great wealth, and abundant in his charities, expending immenſe ſums for almoſt all public objeƈts, and towards numerous individuals. In one inſtance he received a note in which the writer, then at his door, begged his aſſiſtance, intimating that in the failure of his application, he ſhould kill himſelf. The Colonel talked with the young man, and found he had ruined himſelf by gambling. He befriended him, and ultimately ſaved him, not only from the meditated crime, but reſcued him from miſery, and was the means of his becoming a pious and reſpeƈtable perſon.

The Colonel was highly reſpeƈted in life, and died greatly lamented, Feb. 1830, aged 84.

(76.) JOSIAH FALCONER, was a watchmaker, at 143 Cherry ſtreet.

(77.) WALTER BERRY, THEODORUS POLHEMUS, and JEREMIAH JOHNSON, Truſtees and Commiſſioners of the Town of Brooklyn.

(78.) The 13th Regiment (N. Y. Artillery), under command of Lt.-Col. Martin Boerum, who was a reſident of

Brooklyn. To this regiment was attached (at the time of the apprehended attack on Long Iſland and New-York, in 1812) the Brooklyn artillery company, commanded by Capt. Lawrence Brouwer.

(79.) DANIEL D. TOMPKINS, born at Scarſdale, Weſt-cheſter Co., N. Y., June 21, 1774, graduated at Columbia College, in 1795, was admitted to the bar in New-York, in 1797, and ſoon attained a high poſition both in and out of his profeſſion. In 1804, he repreſented New York city in Congreſs, and was appointed an aſſociate juſtice of the Supreme Court of the State. In 1807, he was elected Governor of the State, which office he held, by ſucceſſive re-elections, till 1817, when he was elected Vice-Preſident of the United States. To this latter office he was again elected in 1820, and held it until March 4, 1825, and died on Staten Iſland on the 21ſt of June of the ſame year. He contributed largely, by his exertions and influence, to the national ſuc-ceſs of America in the war of 1812; and, in 1817, recom-mended, in a ſpecial meſſage to the Legiſlature, the total abolition of ſlavery in the State of New-York, which grand and humane purpoſe was fully ſecured by the paſſage of an act which took effect July 4, 1827.

(80.) Hibernian Provident Society. Its officers, at this time, were Robert Swanton, *President;* John McKinley, *First V. Pres.;* Alexander McBeth, *Second V. Pres.;* James Hays, *Treas.;* Ignatius Redmond, *Sec'y,* Henry Eagle, *Assist.;* Robert Moore, Dennis H. Doyle, Cornelius Heeny, Thomas Foote, Doctor Morton, George White, John Craig, *Standing Committee.*

(81.) Supreme Concord Society, No. 1, instituted in 1801, met at Pierson's Porter House, 259 William street, on the last Thursday in every month. Their anniversary was held on Easter Monday. Colin Tomlie was the *R. W. President,* Thomas Duncan, *V. Pres.,* Gairn Spence, *Treas.,* John Mustard, *Sec'y,* and John Strachan, *Master of Ceremonies.* Attached to this was an Order of Merit, which met once a quarter, and held its anniversary on the second Monday in Easter.

(82.) New Market. The present Catharine market, at Catharine slip, New-York, which was finished in 1800, and was properly called, at that time, "the New Market."

(83.) The embarkation, according to an eye-witness, occupied only fifteen minutes.

(84.) Corlear's Hook, foot of Grand ftreet, E. R.

(85.) "There, however, was difplayed a lively mark of female patriotifm and affection, as well as ingenious portray of fancy in the circumftance of arranging a beautiful group of ladies in the train of the *genius of liberty*.—Thefe fair daughters of Columbia gave the tear of fenfibility to the memory of the brave—and exhibited the undiffembling teftimonial of virtuous hearts." *N. Y. Public Adv.*, May 27.

(86.) Benjamin De Witt, M. D., was, in 1807, Profeffor of the Inftitute of Medicine, and Lecturer on Chemiftry, in the College of Phyficians and Surgeons in the City of New-York, to which office he had been appointed by the Regents of the Univerfity. In 1808, he was appointed, by the fame authority, Profeffor of Chemiftry in the fame inftitution, and fubfequently filled the offices, in 1811, of Vice-Prefident and Lecturer on Materia Medica, and in 1813, upon the confolidation of the College of Phyficians and Surgeons and Rutgers Medical School, became Vice-Prefident and Profeffor of Natural and Experimental Philofophy. To Rutgers Medical College he rendered great fervices, particularly in obtaining a liberal grant, from the State, of $30,000. He afterwards became Health Officer of the City of New-York, and while in the difcharge of his official duties, in 1819, contracted the yellow fever at the Quarantine at Staten Ifland, where he died on the 11th day of September, 1819, at the age of 45. He was the author of a differtation on the effect of oxygen gas, which was publifhed in 1797 ; was a man of learning, and of benevolent difpofition.

(87.) THE SCORPION was a floop-of-war, of 16 guns, and probably the fame veffel which (then having 14 guns) was, in 1772, commanded by Lord Keith, then a lieutenant in the Britifh navy. The Scorpion appears in the lift of the navy as early as 1756, and was in the fleet, under Admiral Saunders, at the reduction of Quebec, in 1759, and came out here again at the commencement of the Revolutionary War, but we cannot afcertain exactly when fhe became a prifon-hulk. Philip Freneau was confined in her, in 1780 ; in December of which year her hull was advertifed for fale by the naval ftorekeeper at New-York, but was not purchafed.

(88.) THE STROMBOLO was a fire-fhip, and came out here at the commencement of the Revolution. She was com-manded, when a prifon-fhip, from Auguft 21ft to December

10th, 1780, by Jeremiah Downer, and never had lefs than 150 prifoners, and oftener over 200, on board. She was advertifed for fale, December 6th, 1780 (in which advertifement fhe was ftill mentioned as a fire-fhip), but no purchafer appeared.

(89.) The Hunter was originally a floop-of-war. She was advertifed for fale in December, 1780, but found no purchafer. Capt. Dring (fee his Narrative, p. 71) thinks fhe was mainly ufed as a *ftore-fhip* and medical depôt.

Clofing Note.
(*From the N. Y. Public Advertifer.*)

At the requeft of the Wallabout Committee we have poftponed any further defcription of the late proceffion to the *tomb of the martyrs.* The order of proceffion, the embarkation, the arrival in Brooklyn, and the proceedings at the tomb, with the prayer, oration, &c., is about to be publifhed in pamphlet form, under the direction of a perfon fpecially appointed for the purpofe. It will be printed in the beft manner, and fhall appear without delay. *Phil. Aurora, June 1, 1808.*

www.ingramcontent.com/pod-product-compliance
Lightning Source LLC
Chambersburg PA
CBHW060555030726
47498CB00005B/1402